Help!
Was That A Career Limiting Move?

By
Pamela J. Holland &
Marjorie Brody, CSP, CMC, PCC

Help! Was That A Career Limiting Move?

Copyright 2005
Second Edition
Career Skills Press
Printed in Winfield, KS
United States of America

Edited by: Miryam S. Roddy & Laura Kremp
Cover design by: George Foster & Miryam S. Roddy

Career Skills Press
815 Greenwood Avenue, Suite 8
Jenkintown, PA 19046 USA
Toll free: 800-726-7936
215-886-1688
Fax: 215-886-1699
E-mail: brody@BrodyCommunications.com
www.BrodyCommunications.com or www.MarjorieBrody.com

Library of Congress Control Number: 2004110842

ISBN 1-931148-13-9

Table of Contents

Table of Contents

Table of Contents

Acknowledgements

"To my colleagues past & present and to our clients who teach me every day about the power of good people doing great work. As always, to my husband Stephen, who continues to be my most trusted human resource advisor."

— Pamela Holland

"I want to thank Pam Holland for her loyalty and constant source of creativity; Miryam S. Roddy for her untiring editing; our clients for their examples of CLMs; and to my husband, Alan, for being who he is."

— Marjorie Brody

Foreword

It has been more than three years since the first edition of *Help! Was That A Career Limiting Move?* was published. The world is truly a different place. We received our first printed copies of the book on September 10, 2001 -- hot off the press. On that autumn morning we were full of anticipation and hope about the success of our book and, more importantly, about what the future held for college students and seasoned businesspeople alike.

Stabs to the heart of America and our economy came quickly, fiercely and painfully. No one could have imagined the terror, tragedy and uncertainty that blanketed our nation and work force.

The genesis of the "Help!" book came from our recognition that despite the gangbuster economic growth and the potentially limitless opportunities that awaited even modestly ambitious people -- complacency, sloppiness and arrogance were running rampant as we entered the 21st Century.

Our lectures and book events always reminded people that the book was written with the following quote as its foundation: "Little things don't mean a lot, they mean everything!" In 2001, our audiences gave subtle nods to that concept; as if to say, "OK if you say so, but I think you're making a bigger deal out of it than you need to."

Now, three years later, after corruption, scandal, off shoring, outsourcing and corporate cutbacks have taken the starch out of white-collar and blue-collar workers alike, people are not only paying attention to "the little things," they are starving to understand and master them to set themselves apart from the crowd.

The second edition of *Help! Was That A Career Limiting Move?* was written with the same overall objective in mind: Give people the awareness, tools and motivation to increase success in their professional lives, but deliver the information in a way that is as amusing and quick to absorb as it is practical.

We have added many new stories so that you can learn from others' mistakes. Some CLMs have come from places as visible as the front page of *The Wall Street Journal*, others have been whispered confidentially to us by clients and readers alike. We hope they serve as an eye-opening way to give you the incentive, knowledge and confidence to thrive in these turbulent times.

Here's to your future full of "career enhancing moves!"

Help! Was That a Career Limiting Move?

Introduction

Your GPA rocks (or maybe you just squeezed by), you're a cyberspace genius, your good looks and smooth-talking ways have just earned you the opportunity to work for the company of your dreams. You're hooked up … your success is a shoo-in, right?

Wrong!

Success doesn't just come from technical or academic knowledge or experience. Survival in the "real world" requires knowing — and more importantly, doing — the dozens of little things that make the difference between being viewed as a peon, a dolt or being considered sharp, savvy and a fast-tracker.

We decided to write *Help! Was That A Career Limiting Move?* after thousands of hours spent training and coaching in the boardrooms and mail rooms of every type of company, from *Fortune* 100 corporations to small, family-owned businesses. We were reminded that preventing career limiting moves (CLMs) is something they don't teach you in school. As a matter of fact, the old adage "you don't know what you don't know" is never more appropriate than when it comes to identifying or making a career limiting move.

Help! Was That a Career Limiting Move?

Not surprisingly, many CLMs are often made before someone even has an official job offer. Take the case of a young man we know, Brian, who was in his junior year at Princeton University when he stopped by our office during a semester break. Brian is intelligent and well-read. He is also an extremely kind, thoughtful person. When he asked for some interview advice for an upcoming internship, one of the first things we discussed was the value of writing a memorable thank-you note. As we talked, a look of horror grew on Brian's face. When asked what was wrong, he sheepishly replied, "I have never even thought to write a thank-you note following an interview."

We recently attended a dinner party for a friend, Allan Kimball, who was retiring from his position as president of a semiconductor company. At the party, it was extremely clear that the respect and admiration Allan had garnered during his 25 years with this organization were not merely a result of his technical knowledge or strategic thinking. His reputation as an accomplished leader came from the thoughtful, respectful and considerate way he had always conducted himself — from his first day on the job as an energetic young salesman to his last day as head of the company.

Allan made few CLMs as he climbed the corporate ladder, because he had the knowledge and discipline to practice what we cover in this book.

The principles outlined in this book are timeless. They are rules that Allan and others like him have known and followed throughout their careers. So while your computer, cell phone, Palm Pilot or even your shoe style will likely need updating before you make your first million, the contents of this book will keep you on track from now until someone is raising a toast to you, your accomplishments and contributions.

We can't guarantee that by heeding these same rules and principles that you, too, will be president of a company some day. We can promise, however, that by reading *Help! Was That A Career Limiting Move?* and by putting your newly found knowledge into practice each and every day, your future success and opportunities will be much greater!

Interpersonal Communication

(1)

Are You Ready for "The Trumpster?"

Skip the lights, cameras, action and the intensity of millions of people watching your every move and go straight to the question ...

How ready are you to face the Donald Trumps of the world -- in other words, the countless powerful, opinionated, business savvy, in-control people who help decide your future each and every day?

Unless you were somewhere other than planet Earth from January through April 2004, you were at least aware of or maybe even addicted to the first season of NBC's prime time hit, "The Apprentice." Countless Americans (us included) became immersed in the behavior, politics and study of human nature that played out on our TV screens on a weekly basis, pulsing to the beat of "Money, Money, Money."

Whether you are a Donald devotee like Sam Solovey, the ousted contestant in the series premiere, who offered Donald $250,000 for the privilege of working for him, or someone who sneers at the mention of the Trump name while visions of a megalomaniac dance through your head; there's no denying that "The Apprentice" offered up a cornucopia of lessons in business success and survival.

Even as the show emphasized leadership and management ability at board-room levels, it brought to life the importance of loyalty, reliability, creativity, determination and strong communication skills -- for entry-level success as well as for executive power & privilege.

Below are our picks for key lessons learned:

- A relentless passion to make your company and boss successful will get you noticed.

- Think smart AND work hard. One without the other won't get you any-where close to the boardroom.

- Credentials, like a finely tailored suit, may help you in the beginning, but how you wear them is what counts in the end.

- You will be successful to the degree that others want you to be successful.

- Surround yourself with individuals who are capable, honest and fair. Keep your distance from those who aren't, or if you have the authority, fire them.

- There is a fine line between optimism and wishful thinking. Don't ever be complacent.

- Confidence, communication and credibility are 3 C's with enduring value greater than the finest cut diamond.

How do *you* measure up?

Finally, do you have a passion? Do you have a plan? Do you have a sense of what you have and want to offer? We're certain Mr. Trump doesn't just wake up each day and wait for things to happen.

Neither should you.

(2)

Yo dude – let's start with some basics

If you don't take the time to acknowledge people, chances are that others will be much less likely to acknowledge you. This applies to both the daily aspects of your work life as well as to your potential for career advancement.

A person we know once asked, "How many times do you have to say 'Hello' or 'Hi' to someone you are continually seeing in the hallway or office?" It isn't something you count – it's something you do. People want to be acknowledged – it's a sign of respect. If you see someone over and over again in a day, you can start the day with "Good morning," "Hi" or "Hello." The second time you see the person, you can use one of these greetings again. As you continually see this person, you don't have to speak, but you *do* have to nod, smile or make eye contact in recognition of his or her presence.

When you leave a meeting, or at the end of the day, you also need to let people know you are going by saying "Goodbye."

Remember, however, that in most professional environments, it's not appropriate to say "Whazzzzup," "S'up," "Word" or "Yo."

(3)

Pleased to meet ya!

Business etiquette is one of the most widely requested training programs our company, Brody Communications Ltd., offers. At the beginning of each program, participants are asked what specific skills they hope to improve as a result of the session. The most frequently stated desire of our attendees is, "I need help making introductions!" So, if you feel the same way, you are not alone.

Remember these introduction basics and you won't be left "out in the cold."

When standing with someone who fails to introduce you …

- You can extend your hand and say: "I am (<u>put your name here</u>). I don't believe we've met." Or, "I am (<u>put your name here</u>), and you are?"

When you want to introduce someone, but you've forgotten his or her name …

- You can say to the person whose name you forgot, "I don't believe you've met (<u>put the other person's name here</u>)," or "Have you met (<u>put the other person's name here</u>)?" At that point, the person whose name you forgot will probably give his or her name, completing the introduction for you.

Help! Was That a Career Limiting Move?

When making introductions …

- Say the name of the highest-ranking person (your boss, customer, etc.) first.

- Mention the other person's name and say something about him or her.

- Go back to the first person and again say his or her name and something about him or her.

  Here's an example: "Tom, I want you to meet Julie Smith, who works in the HR department. Julie, Tom Sullivan is our client from XYZ Company."

When responding to an introduction, use the name that was given in the introduction: Richard – not Rich; Marjorie – not Margie. Don't use nicknames unless that is how people refer to themselves.

(4)

Be aware of invisible red ink!

Remember back in school, when your teachers would mark up your papers with red ink when you misspelled words or used a colon when you should have used a semicolon? Well, you might not have a teacher marking your business papers, but you do have colleagues, management and even clients who are making judgments about you based on your e-mails, letters and other written documents.

The quality of your written communication says a lot about you, your commitment to doing excellent work and your attention to detail.

Don't be lazy! Take the time to let your computer do the checking. But don't rely on the computer spell-check function for catching grammar mistakes or word usage errors. ALWAYS take a minute to double-check your document – or have another person do so before it is sent. Reading it out loud is the best way to catch mistakes.

When it comes to the name of a person or company, make sure you double-check the accuracy of your spelling. Is the person's name Kathy or Cathy? Is the company's name Andersen or Anderson? Never assume. People really get turned off or feel insulted if you don't take the time to get it right.

One misspelled word could stand between you and a sought-after job, promotion or sale.

CLM Flash: 2004 - According to a survey by the College Board's National Commission on Writing, a majority of U.S. employers say about one-third of workers do not meet the writing requirements of their position.

(5)

To make a long story short …

Do you know people who ramble on and on? If you do, it's probably tempting to cut them off, put them on mute or delete their voice mails.

You may even avoid their work areas, especially when you're busy, for fear that even the simplest exchange may lead to a never-ending story or explanation.

Once you stop to think about people you know who talk too much, be honest with yourself and consider whether that description applies to you, too. If you think it does, it's time to learn how to get your point across using fewer words.

Think through what you want to say. Exactly what is the point? Once you've determined that, what do you need to say to back up your point? Then, how do you say it succinctly?

Make sure you don't send long-winded voice mails. Listen to messages before sending them. Do you unnecessarily repeat your point more than once? Is it clear what you are trying to convey or does the heart of your message get lost in irrelevant stuff that surrounds it? Listen, erase and record again until your message is crisp, clear and concise … the kind of message you wouldn't mind picking up if you had only two minutes to run and catch a plane.

Earning the reputation of someone who "gets to the point" is valuable. People are more likely to ask your opinion. Better yet, they will listen to what you have to say.

(6)

So enough about me. Why don't you talk about me?

People who are not prepared to chat or create interesting conversation, or who only talk about themselves, are BORING!!

Here are some tips for preparing yourself to be a good conversationalist:

- Ask open-ended questions. Start with "What," "How" and "Why."

- Be a good listener.

- Read all sections of at least one newspaper a day (*USA Today* can be your *Cliff Notes* for current events) or one good news magazine a week. Suggestions: *Fortune, Fast Company, Inc., Newsweek, Time, BusinessWeek.* You can also read "fun" stuff like *People, Cosmo, Men's Health, Rolling Stone,* etc. Don't forget to read best-selling business books and general bestsellers.

- Observe what is going on around you.

Topics that Work

- Weather

- Traffic
- Common experiences
- Current events
- Travel
- Hobbies
- Books
- Movies
- Children
- Pets
- Sports
- Work
- TV Shows

Topics to Avoid

- Your health or others' health
- Controversial issues
- Cost of items
- Topics of a sexual nature
- Personal misfortunes
- Gossip
- Stories of questionable taste or dirty jokes
- Politics
- Religion

(7)

Don't crowd me

Has anyone ever told you or looked at you as if to say, "Hey, you're in my space?" Maybe you're the one who has wanted to say that to someone else. Either way, an individual's personal space is something that must be recognized and respected.

When you talk to others, don't get too close. In the United States, typically 3 to 4 feet is an appropriate distance. The rules may vary in other cultures, so if you're traveling abroad or interacting with people from other countries, make it a point to find out what is considered acceptable and act accordingly.

Invading someone's space may not only be considered rude, it may be considered harassment, especially if you are in contact with someone of the opposite sex. Inappropriate touching or closeness might be construed as harassment, and is absolutely not tolerated in corporate America.

When in doubt, err on the side of being conservative. Here are some things to keep in mind:

- Avoid standing directly behind people when they sit at their computers.

- Never take something from a person's desk without asking.

- Don't hang in the doorway of someone's office or cubicle while he or she is on the phone.

- When you walk into an office or cubicle, remain standing unless invited to sit.

- Don't shake your finger or point at anyone.

Consideration and respect for others should be your overall guideline. If you stay mindful of this, chances are very good that you won't have to worry about inappropriately "crossing the line."

(8)

I like the way you talk

If you ever watched the long-running TV sitcom "Friends" during the time when Chandler was dating Janice (the woman with the high, nasally voice and laugh that could make anyone's skin crawl) then you've already had a taste of the negative impact someone's voice quality can have. Janice may have been bright, capable and a wonderful person, but it was hard to notice any of those redeeming qualities while wincing every time she spoke.

If you have no idea who Janice is, or didn't watch "Friends," then think for a moment about someone whose voice turned you off. Was the person's voice too high, or too soft? Was the person mumbling or speaking so slowly that you wondered whether he or she really understood what you were saying or was capable of taking care of your problem?

People make judgments about you just by listening to your voice. It isn't only the words you use, but *how* you say them that can make a difference.

When people see you (face-to-face communication), the impact of your voice is approximately 38% of the overall impression you make – the "picture." Over the phone, it jumps to 85% — since there are no visual cues.

There are certain things you can do to have a more pleasing voice:

- **Have an appropriate expression.** Sound enthusiastic, or, when appropriate, alter your tone to fit the conversation (sounding sympathetic when talking about sad news, etc.).

- **Speak slowly enough** that people understand you easily, yet not so slowly that you take too long to complete a thought. This rate will vary throughout the country.

- **Pause.** By pausing, you give people enough time to take in what you are saying. When you finish a thought, think of adding a period (.) by counting to three in your mind. If it would be a colon (:) , count to two, and if it is a comma (,) , count to one. In other words, don't run your words together.

- **Eliminate fillers** – "uh," "um," "OK" and "you know."

- **Speak loud enough to be easily heard.** Speaking in a whisper is non-assertive and annoying. If people ask you to speak up or to repeat yourself, this is a clue that you need help in this area.

- **Speak softly enough to avoid shouting and screaming.** If people are asking you to "shh" or lower your tone, that's a clue, too.

- **When on the phone, have a mirror that you can see nearby and keep a smile on your face when you talk.** Your voice also will reflect the smile.

- **Watch your diction.** Completing words makes you sound smarter. Things like saying the "ing" ending can make a difference ("going" not "gonna," "doing," not "doin'"). Another problem is dropping the beginning of words ("them," not "'em").

- **Control your breathing** when you get nervous or excited. It helps to lower your pitch, making you sound more credible. Learn how to breathe from the diaphragm, not your chest. It helps you project your voice more easily.

The best way to assess your own voice is to tape-record yourself or listen to your voice-mail messages. Decide what you need to practice so you sound better in face-to-face encounters and electronically.

Additional distracting speaking styles we've coached people to improve include mumbling and covering their mouths with hands while talking. This tends to happen particularly when a person is nervous or defensive. Keep your hands away from your mouth when speaking and don't swallow words or let your voice trail off with any thoughts. Seek the help of a trusted friend or co-worker who is willing to signal you when you start doing any of these bad habits.

The power of your voice is the sum of its vocal quality and the words you choose. You must not take either for granted to ensure that your speaking formula is a winning combination.

(9)

Come again?

There is an old expression, "It's better to sit quietly and be thought a fool than to open your mouth and remove all doubt." We suspect these words of wisdom were first uttered for the benefit of someone who had difficulty listening.

Beyond the fact that it is common courtesy and a sign of respect to be a good listener, it is also true that many of the most successful individuals in business do far more listening than talking.

You can become a more effective listener by adopting four key habits:

- **Try to be a patient listener by taking a mental breather.** Don't just wait for a chance to add your two cents when another person is through talking. Listen instead of trying to fill the "void." Genuinely interested people convey a sense of respect by not making assumptions about what other people are thinking.

- **Avoid cutting off someone's last words in a rush to respond.** This is important for two reasons: First, the speaker will feel better about you as a considerate person and listener. Second, you may learn that your knee-jerk response was the worst thing you could have added to the conversation.

- **Listen with more than your ears.** Effective listening involves the eyes and entire body. Making eye contact helps convey sincerity. By nodding your head occasionally, your listening will be seen as active, not passive. Be mindful of your body language as well. When listening, posture is key. Good listeners sit up and lean forward when others are speaking to them.

- **Eliminate distractions** such as the phone or clutter that may be surrounding you. But, don't get too comfortable. You want to stay poised for action and prevent your mind from drifting.

Listening skills are especially critical in doing a job accurately, promoting teamwork, fostering good client relationships and being perceived as respectful and truly interested.

Anyone can learn to listen more effectively by making the commitment to practice the listening skills covered here. Also, invite a couple of people you trust to provide feedback on your progress.

When you truly listen, you learn … more than you ever thought possible.

(10)

It's all in the wrist

Giving a friend a high-five may be OK in the gym, but it isn't standard for an official business greeting. The handshake is the recognized form of greeting in most business situations. Learn how to do it well.

Here are some guidelines to keep in mind:

- Extend your hand to someone when you are approximately one arm's length away (2 to 4 feet in American culture, which can vary elsewhere).

- Make sure your thumb is up and you connect thumb joint to thumb joint. None of that grab-the-fingers stuff!

- Clasp firmly (both genders), not bone crushing, however. Then pump one to three times and release.

Things to be careful about:

- Carry all things – drinks, briefcases, etc. – in your left hand, so you are always prepared to shake.

- Keep your hands dry.

- If someone doesn't respond, drop your hand – it could be for religious reasons.

- If someone doesn't have a usable right arm or hand, extend your left, but *do* still extend.

Remember, fish-like handshakes give a wimpy impression. Don't let that be your hallmark.

CLM Flash: Employers responding to Job Outlook 2001, an annual survey of employers' hiring intentions as they relate to new college graduates, showed that a candidate's handshake had more influence than in-your-face attributes such as body piercing, visible tattoos and unusual hairstyles.

(11)

Step up to the plate

You don't have control over every situation. You *do* have control over how you respond. There are three general types of people:

- **The Passive Person**
  - ✓ gives in all the time.
  - ✓ gives his or her rights to others.
  - ✓ usually demonstrates poor eye contact and has a soft voice.

- **The Aggressive Person**
  - ✓ takes away the rights of others.
  - ✓ says it's "My way or the highway."
  - ✓ usually has a loud voice, stares people down and gestures a lot.

- **The Assertive Person**
  - ✓ stands up for self – but not at the expense of others.
  - ✓ is firm and uses specific examples/facts rather than emotions to support opinions.

Most experts would agree, as we do, that assertive behavior creates the most productive working atmosphere. Yet, many people find it difficult to act assertively.

No one likes a bully – not as a child and not as an adult. If you find yourself having aggressive tendencies, chill out.

Being aggressive may appear to be getting you what you want. In reality, it only builds a sense of fear or dislike in others around you. Watch your voice (volume and tone), avoid intimidating or hostile gestures and don't launch a personal attack against anyone. You will express yourself better if you are calm, fair and specific.

If you tend to be passive, chances are you still get frustrated by letting others dominate you. On the surface, you may seem agreeable – underneath you may be fostering resentment or developing a victim mentality. Don't let it happen! It's not healthy for you or the organization. Use specific examples to support your opinion. Try to be factual, not emotional, and stand up for what you believe in.

(12)

You may not be Jim Carrey or Chris Rock, but …

Your sense of humor can make your work life more enjoyable and actually motivate people around you. In our intense, pressure-packed and high-speed world, laughter may be one of the best energizers and stress busters out there. Walt Disney said, "Take what you do seriously, but not yourself." How very true. People who can laugh at themselves are better liked and live longer.

This doesn't mean that you should strive for a reputation as a joke teller. It also doesn't mean that you should put down others. The best guideline is to keep your laughter and humor in check when it is at the direct expense of someone else or when it could be detrimental to you and your organization's credibility and perceived integrity.

Never tell jokes or use humor about the following possibly sensitive subjects:

- Age
- Race
- Gender
- Ethnicity
- Sexual preference

- Religion
- Specific company rules or departments

You should, however, be open to finding the humor in your own slip-ups and personality quirks as well as in some chaotic or difficult situations. Laughter relaxes people and reduces tension. Find a reason to laugh. It certainly can put things into perspective.

CLM Flash: Question -- Did you know what is the most popular TV episode of all time? *Answer* -- "The Mary Tyler Moore Show" when Mary couldn't contain herself at Chuckles the clown's funeral.

(13)

Well, since you asked …

No one ever said that constructive criticism is easy to handle, but we all know that asking for and receiving feedback is key to personal and professional growth. When people (your manager or others) take the time to let you know how you're doing, be grateful for their thoughts and comments even if you don't like what they say.

What you don't know can hurt you, so take an active role in increasing the quality and quantity of comments and suggestions you receive to improve your performance.

Start by setting time aside with your manager and tell him or her that you are always open to feedback about the way you are doing your job. Don't be afraid to ask, "What could I have done better?" Or, "Would you have done it the same way?" If you are passed up for a promotion, ask what you need to do differently.

Typically, performance feedback is easier to get than comments on more subjective things like grooming, dress, image and networking. If you can't get feedback from your manager, ask valued colleagues and friends. You might not always like what you hear, but at least you will not be in the dark.

It is important for you to get input on your performance, teamwork, dedication and professionalism from people above and below you in the company's hierarchy. It is equally critical for you to seek the same from clients, vendors and co-workers and virtually anyone you come in contact with during your workday.

Make no mistake about it, like most things in your career, you are the one ultimately responsible for obtaining and using the feedback necessary to enhance your performance. Invite others to give you feedback, receive it respectfully and demonstrate that you are willing to make the necessary changes in your behavior. This lets everyone know that the process was not a waste of time or energy … for you or them.

(14)

Thanks for the compliment!

Mark Twain said he could live for three weeks on a good compliment. Everyone loves to be recognized for his or her contributions, ideas, hard work and willingness to be a team player. Yet, how often do you compliment others? It's probably a lot less than you might think.

Unfortunately, many people find it easier to criticize colleagues or bosses than to appreciate what they offer. Not only can this be counterproductive, it can create an atmosphere that doesn't foster creativity or innovation. Many a notable career has been launched by the person who is patient, open-minded and takes the time to respect and acknowledge others.

Go out of your way to look for opportunities to recognize others. Let these people know how much you appreciate them. One vice president we know used to encourage his sales managers to "catch people doing something right." This can be done in person, on the phone or via e-mail.

It takes awhile to get into the habit, but the results of giving praise are well worth the effort. First, you become more positive – looking for what is good in others. Second, you make someone else feel valued. Finally, you will distinguish yourself as a pleasant and supportive colleague. This could be one of the most valuable contributions you make to your organization.

CLM Flash: Try this exercise to increase the number of compliments you give in a day. Put five pennies in your right pocket each morning. Each time you compliment someone, put one penny into your left pocket. At the end of the day, the goal is to have all the change in your left pocket.

(15)

All this and you're modest, too

It doesn't matter if you were hired for big bucks or at entry level for minimum wage, ultimately you are only worth what you contribute. Even if the job market may be hot, it doesn't mean things will stay that way. You must produce and you must be the kind of person others want to be around.

Where does humility fit in? Many people get confused about when to be humble and when it's appropriate to toot their own horn. As a general rule, interviews and performance appraisals are the key times when you can put modesty aside.

Don't hold back on your accomplishments, contributions, risks you have taken or kudos you have received. Do balance that information by being prepared to give specifics and by acknowledging those who helped you along the way. It is more than OK to share the wealth with others on your team as long as you do not skip over or diminish the true role you played. These are not the times to be self-effacing.

On an ongoing basis, make sure your manager is aware of your contributions – don't just assume that he/she realizes all you do. Keep in touch with him or her regularly, giving updates as things occur.

Above all, don't be arrogant. Become a team player and a contributor. Not only will your company benefit from the synergy you help create by working effectively with others, but you will quickly develop a reputation as someone who is confident, fair and great to work with.

(16)

Sticks and stones ...

It is never easy to be verbally attacked. The immediate inclination of most individuals may be to respond in kind, which only escalates the situation.

Maintaining your composure and dignity may not be easy, but it is the right and smart thing to do. When emotions get out of control, so do sensibilities. Things said in anger are rarely productive and often come back to haunt the person who said them.

Here is a good formula to follow should someone verbally attack you:

- Let the person vent – without responding. Be sure to listen to what the person is and isn't saying.

- Once he or she has stopped talking, paraphrase what the person said and how you think he or she feels: "You sound angry that I mailed the letter late."

- Probe – ask questions to get a real handle on what issue exists. By now, the person will be calmer, because you listened and acknowledged his or her feelings, and be more likely to answer logically.

• Now, you can problem solve or refute logically.

Always determine if an argument is worth winning. Sometimes, it's better to let things go. As the old Kenny Rogers' song goes, "Know when to hold 'em, know when to fold 'em, know when to walk away, know when to run."

How many times have you or someone you know said something in the heat of the moment that could not be taken back? Keep your cool, don't engage in unproductive exchanges and stay focused on your objectives. Not only will you ultimately save yourself enormous aggravation, but you will establish a reputation as a mature and decent human being.

(17)

But on the other hand …

The ability to reach a conclusion in a timely fashion is important in the business world. But reaching a conclusion and jumping to conclusions are not the same.

Making a sound decision requires getting the necessary information, doing an analysis and considering alternatives. Jumping to conclusions can lead to embarrassment or inappropriate action.

Don't let preconceived ideas or stereotypes cloud your decision making. Be open-minded to others' views and possible alternatives. Resist the urge to pass judgment on a project or person based on hearsay.

There is also great value in considering the ideas, feelings and opinions of others before you make your mind up. People who make a conscious effort to recognize multiple sides to a story or situation are less likely to be blindsided and more likely to be considered fair and wise.

(18)

It's Greek to me

Nothing turns people off quicker than not understanding what you're saying. Think of the times when someone used language that left you out in the cold. Was this person using acronyms or jargon that only a few could understand? Was his or her vocabulary full of obscure, rarely used words that may have only been understood by a college English professor?

If you have ever been with someone who communicates that way, you probably felt uncomfortable, irritated and less than impressed. Don't end up speaking in a way that turns people off. Here are some examples of what to avoid:

- humor that people don't understand, inside jokes or stories
- pretentious words (so large that people are running to grab a dictionary)
- technical jargon to non-technical people
- buzzwords or acronyms that others don't know
- name-dropping

In order for others to appreciate you and what you have to offer, you must be able to connect with them verbally. Using clear and considerate language speaks volumes.

(19)

Don't let the door hit you on the way out

You have lots of opportunities to "show up" at meetings, events or client/colleague offices. Arriving on time is important. It shows respect. But knowing when to leave is just as important.

Always have an exit strategy. Typically, at the end of a meeting, it's "go back to work." At an event (party, etc.) don't be the last one out, holding up the host or planners.

Also, be very aware of lingering in someone else's office or cubicle. Stay alert for nonverbal indicators that the person wants you to leave (standing up, looking at the computer, turning away from you, etc.). If the person receives a phone call when you're there, exit gracefully without interrupting the call.

If you see that someone is busy, or needs to work, it's time to show yourself to the door!

On the flip side, if you find yourself getting interrupted or stuck by someone who is oblivious to your need to get to work, don't be afraid to politely let the person know. Say something like, "I wish I had more time to talk, but right now I have a deadline on the XYZ project and need to give it all of my attention."

CLM Flash: Is there someone you know or work with who chronically takes up your time and is oblivious to your cues about leaving your office? When possible, ask to meet in this person's work space. Then you will have greater control when you want the interaction to end.

(20)

All for one and one for all!

T-E-A-M ... Go Team! Depending on the size of your organization, teams are generally set up for a variety of reasons, including diversity, technology, life and work balance, integration (when mergers and acquisitions take place) and sports teams. A wonderful way to get known within your organization and connect with people you wouldn't otherwise meet is to get involved in initiatives and activities outside of your immediate area of responsibility.

Talk to people within your department or within human resources. See what opportunities exist. We know of many young employees who found excellent mentors and advocates because they played golf or baseball or served on the diversity team.

Associations are also great ways to participate and work with others. Whatever field or industry your job is in, there is probably a professional association you can join. By joining associations, you experience new opportunities for networking, obtain additional learning experiences, etc., with others in your same field. For example, if you are in the purchasing department, there is the Purchasing Management Association. If you are an accountant, there is the Institute of Management Accountants.

By joining associations and other work-related teams, you will learn more about your chosen field. What a great way to meet others, as well. If you do need a resource, this is the way to ensure there are always plenty of people you can contact.

Joining is only the beginning of team and association participation. After you are comfortable, start to become more actively involved. Look for opportunities to take leadership roles. When you give your time, energy and full commitment to teams or associations, chances are you will get back much more than you gave.

(21)

I'll call you …

Follow-up is the only way to build relationships and create advocates. You will meet hundreds, if not thousands, of people throughout your life. Some will have a large impact and others a small effect.

Many of these people can make a difference in your career … if you stay in touch. It's not necessary to call people daily, yet a periodic phone call or e-mail keeps the door open. All too often we wait until we need people before reconnecting – not a good move.

Even now, think of people you knew in high school, college or a previous job – people you lost touch with. Find them and reconnect. Let them know what you are doing; find ways to help them.

If you meet someone and exchange names and cards, and promise to reconnect … do it! It only takes a minute to send an e-mail or note to follow up. The impression you make will last longer than the time you invest.

Relationships are built over time; developing advocates takes awhile. But during this time frame, always keep in touch. You never know who may be helpful or who you may influence and help as you move through your career and life.

(22)

Mi casa, su casa

During your career, you will have many opportunities to host visitors at your company's facilities and travel to client sites and other meetings out of the office. It's important to know the proper business behaviors when faced with such encounters – so there's no embarrassing moments or faux pas.

When you have visitors come to your office, never keep them waiting. After the guest arrives, you or an assistant should escort him or her to your office or other meeting room. If taking an elevator, hold the door for the visitor; he or she goes in first. If it's a revolving door, the host enters first, so you can lead the way on the other side.

Another critical component when meeting a visitor relates to the introduction. Greet the person with a firm handshake and smile. If an assistant has brought the visitor to your office, stand and come from behind the desk before shaking hands. If you want your guest to sit, indicate where he or she should sit. You can begin your conversation with small talk, but stick to about three to four minutes of this before diving into the business at hand.

Even though you're still in the office, don't accept calls or interruptions when a scheduled visitor is present, unless it's an emergency.

When the meeting is over, walk your visitor back to the reception area. Say, "I appreciated your visit." If the guest lingers and you need to move on to other business, say, "I'm sorry, I have another meeting to attend." Or, use an assistant to remind you of your next appointment.

If you visit other offices or attend off-site meetings, arrive on time or a few minutes early. When you get there, give your name, company name and name of the person you are visiting to the receptionist. Also present a business card. When the host takes you to his or her office, wait to be told where to sit.

Put your briefcase or purse on the floor. Do not take any candy or other food items that may be visible, unless offered. Wait to be shown where to hang your coat. Remember, the host always takes the lead, unless you called the meeting. If your host takes a call, motion whether you should stay or leave – he or she may desire privacy. If a person enters the room, stand. When it's time to leave, stand, shake hands and thank your host for the visit. Don't overstay your visit. Depending on the type of meeting, write a thank-you note when you return to your office.

Know Your Business

(1)

Will they like me?

Ah, vying for the job of your dreams …

Probably one of the most anxiety-producing and exciting challenges you will face during the course of your professional life. Whether you are being considered for a new job or a new position within your existing company, being granted an interview is only a very small part of the selection process.

Typically, the basic elements of competing for a position include:

- **Creating a dynamic and attention-grabbing cover letter.** In our opinion, this component is one of the most overlooked essentials of the process.

  A cover letter serves as your introduction until you earn the right to introduce yourself in person. Be sure to tailor the letter to the position at hand, noting your accomplishments, objectives and why you believe you are a great match.

- **Make sure that your résumé is thoroughly and professionally written.** There are many books devoted to this. We suggest you buy one. You can also get information on résumés from career-related Web sites like

Monster.com, which has a Resume Center (http://resume.monster.com) that contains tips for writing effective résumés based on the type of industry you are pursuing a career in, addressing previous work-related problems in them, and much more. Always have at least two businesspeople who you respect review your final draft for comments and to make sure that there are no mistakes – spelling, grammar, etc.

- **Be ready for the many companies that conduct telephone interviews.** Keep a record of the positions that you have applied for in a handy place, so when a job-related call comes, you are prepared to reiterate the points made in your cover letter. It will also demonstrate your enthusiasm and commitment if you readily recall key aspects of the company and specific job.

  Always answer your phone in a polite and efficient manner. Make sure that your answering machine or voice mail also reflects your ability to communicate professionally. Keep in mind that the cool and creative message you recorded for your buddies will NOT be received with the same level of amusement by prospective employers.

- **Be prepared for your interview.**

  ✓ Know exactly where you need to be and when. Plan to arrive five to 10 minutes early.

  ✓ Know the company you are interviewing with – check out its Web site, annual reports, etc.

✓ Familiarize yourself with the position and, if unclear, be sure to ask how your performance will be measured.

✓ Be prepared to give specific examples to support the skills, qualities and accomplishments you claim to have.

✓ Your outfit should be business professional. That means a suit, unless you specifically are told that the culture is such that you should wear something else. When in doubt, it is always better to be overdressed than underdressed. Be well-groomed and make sure that your shoes are clean/polished and are in good condition overall.

✓ Demonstrate that you are a good listener by answering questions as they were asked. If unsure, it is OK to paraphrase and repeat the question as you understood it, to make certain that you are clear on what is being asked BEFORE you answer. This will also buy you some additional time if you need it to formulate your response.

✓ Ask the interviewer good questions. Ask for a description of the corporate culture, what characteristics the interviewer believes the ideal candidate should have, how performance is measured, and what are some of the greatest challenges and possible rewards associated with the position.

At the close of the interview, you should concisely summarize why you feel you are the best candidate for the job. Ask about next steps and repeat your interest.

- **Write a thank-you note *immediately* after the interview.** Choose one or two key areas of interest or abilities that you feel are particularly well-suited to the position, especially if you were further enlightened by the interviewer. Always thank the person(s) for his or her time. A handwritten note is best.

Above all else, don't pretend to be someone you are not. Even if you are successful at fooling someone in the interview (and you rarely will be), it means they are hiring someone other than who you really are. The result is eventual disappointment for both of you.

There are many resources that provide further tips on acing the job interview. One can be found on http://interview.monster.com, where in addition to a variety of articles on this subject, visitors can actually put themselves through mock interview scenarios based on desired industry – answering questions and getting rated based on answers chosen.

CLM Flash: Don't be a stalker! There's a difference between showing that you're eager for a position and being an unrelenting pain in the neck. Respect the process & the timelines you're given. Proper restraint will show consideration and good judgement.

(2)

Know your business inside and out

Granted, when you start a new job, it takes some time to "get it." But, the most valuable employees are those whose number one priority is to become experts in their current jobs. They know exactly what the job is – why it is important and how it fits into the bigger picture of the company's vision and mission. If you don't know, ask questions, observe others, be a student.

Clearly, it is critical to be knowledgeable about the company you work for. What is the company's mission? What are its values? Who are the leaders? What are the politics? Spend some time reading, REALLY reading, the corporate literature, Web sites, promotional materials and annual reports.

In today's marketplace, some industries are expanding and others are consolidating. What about *your* industry? To be a valuable employee, it helps to know about your industry and your competition. After all, it is your future. By reading newsletters and trade journals and by attending industry-specific meetings, you will be better equipped to add value and to make wise career decisions.

Layoffs, mergers and directional changes often surprise people who aren't knowledgeable about their jobs, companies and industries. There are very few surprises for proactive, knowledgeable and informed employees.

Having a clear and complete picture of what your organization is all about will set you apart from others. It will give you the perspective you need to make more meaningful contributions, and it will demonstrate to others who work with you that you have initiative and commitment to your company beyond your job description.

(3)

Don't burn bridges

Have you ever heard the expression, "Reputation is everything?" It is not surprising that this saying has been around for as long as we can remember. The quality of a person's reputation is directly related to the quality of relationships that individual has established. This is true not just for the short term or in good times, but for the long run and when challenges might reveal someone of lesser character.

There are many clichés about this topic, including: "Don't cut off your nose to spite your face," "You may win the battle, but lose the war," "Patience is a virtue," "What goes around, comes around" and of course, "Don't burn bridges." While these expressions may seem corny or overused, you will be wise to give them careful thought as you undoubtedly will be tempted to ignore all of them during your career. Avoid the temptation to do so.

Although the list is endless, here are some things to be careful about.

- Don't gossip.
- Don't blame others.
- Do your fair share.
- If you borrow money (in general, not a good idea), be sure to pay it back.

Help! Was That a Career Limiting Move?

- Do what you say you will do.
- Keep in touch with people.
- Don't cheat or steal.
- Don't act in a vengeful way.
- Don't embellish the truth or lie.
- Don't talk disparagingly about your competitors.
- If you switch jobs, don't bad-mouth your old employer or co-workers.
- Don't have an affair or openly flirt with co-workers.
- Keep promises and confidential information confidential.
- Don't use vulgar language or tell racist, sexist or off-color jokes.
- Don't discuss your sex life with colleagues.

We do not believe for a moment that following this list will be easy or that you won't make mistakes along the way. However, we strongly encourage you to regularly review these pointers and challenge yourself to make improvements where needed. Guaranteed, doing this is something you will never regret!

CLM Flash: "It helps with your customers, suppliers and employees. Your reputation is everything, and should be protected at any cost." – David Glass, former CEO, Wal-Mart

(4)

What's the deal with mentoring?

According to the dictionary, mentor means "a wise, loyal advisor" and "to teach or coach ... to advise."

Look around your company and industry. Who do you admire? Who do you identify with in terms of how you would like to conduct yourself in business? Who has attained a level of professional and personal success that you believe you would like to model?

What are some of the particular challenges you are currently facing in your job and at your company? Who do you know who could help you navigate tough situations effectively and help with your overall development in the process?

Answering these questions will help you take the first step toward developing a valuable mentoring relationship.

You do not need to limit yourself to one individual. There may be a couple of people who can help you in different key areas of your professional growth. Mentors can be your allies or advocates. They can be individuals who help you sort things out when faced with complicated situations or company politics, and people who help educate you in the ways of your business – in a subtle and direct way.

Look for opportunities to develop relationships with the people who you identify as possible mentors. Let them get to know a little bit about you and your goals. Ask if these individuals would be willing to mentor you and tell them why they were chosen as well as how you feel they could help you. If they agree, be certain to let them know how appreciative you are and how respectful of their time you will be.

The person being mentored has the responsibility of setting up meetings, doing any assignments, seeking feedback and showing gratitude for the relationship.

A strong mentoring relationship can be one of the most valuable and enduring memories of a person's career. As you grow and practice the rules in this book, you may find yourself looking up from your desk one day only to see someone asking you to be his or her mentor. What a great way to build a legacy!

(5)

Don't get trampled in the mosh pit

Organizational charts are documents that outline an employee's role and reporting structure. In the past, these charts were considered fairly hierarchical, also known as vertical. There has been a tendency over the past decade for some companies to "flatten" out their organizational structures with less clearly delineated lines of authority. It is important to understand these structures and the formal and informal rules that govern the politics of where you work, regardless of which type of organization you work for.

Politics are everywhere. Your place of employment (and that of your clients/customers) is no different. It is important to understand the politics so you can successfully navigate a variety of possible situations that may include …

- **Restructuring** – don't align yourself with just one key player. Be aware of others who have a significant role in the organization so that when restructuring occurs, you have more than one advocate to watch your back.

- **Mergers and acquisitions** – these situations may seem entirely out of your control. However, if you build a cross section of allies and look for a broad range of ways to contribute to your company beyond your specific job description, you will increase your odds of not being chewed up and spit out.

- **Power plays** – there may be times when your manager is in competition with another company manager. Be careful not to get sucked into others' power struggles. Remain honest and loyal to your boss by doing your job the very best you can. Don't be tempted to play the game with them.

It is also very important to clearly understand who reports to whom. It would be inappropriate, for example, for you to go above your manager with information or complaints. Always work with the correct person in order to accomplish something without stepping on toes.

Above all else, be alert to what is going on around you in your organization while remaining focused on your objectives and responsibilities. This should keep you safely above the crowd and positioned to enjoy the ride without getting squashed.

(6)

What are you afraid of?

Even if you're not the type to go sky diving this weekend, or have no intention of going down the Snake River in a kayak, risk taking can be good for business and great for personal and professional growth.

Many of you may have heard of or read *Who Moved My Cheese?* by Spencer Johnson, M.D. One of the key points in this best-selling book was a question not a statement. The question was, "What would you do if you were not afraid?"

Think of opportunities that surround you in your professional and personal life. What is holding you back from doing more and being more of the person you want to be?

Answer the question for yourself: What would you do if you weren't afraid?

Consider the endless possibilities, look to others you trust and respect, give yourself permission to fail, give yourself permission to give it your best shot. Now, go for it!

(7)

Don't straddle the fence

While there's a lot to be said for being diplomatic, there is a fine line between diplomacy and appearing to be void of independent rational thought.

You will inevitably be asked to give your opinion on controversial and seemingly simple matters throughout your career. It is therefore important that you have an opinion. You must be able to explain this opinion logically, clearly and succinctly. Always understand why the person asked, and who he or she is, so that you frame your answer in the appropriate context.

Keep in mind that there may be occasions when you are asked your opinion on a subject not to see whether you give a right or wrong answer, but rather to judge how you think. Your thought process and ability to present your opinion in a compelling way may sometimes supersede the thought itself.

In order to truly succeed in an organization, you need to have your own ideas and know how to convey them effectively and appropriately. Here's a good formula to help you give your point of view in a concise and convincing way.

P – Point of View. State your perspective or opinion about something.

R – Reason. You need to support your point of view with a reason.

E – Explanation or Example. Be very specific when explaining your point of view or providing an example. Be concise, yet still informative.

P – Point of View. End your conversation or presentation by restating your point of view. This helps let your listener know you're done and also prevents you from rambling.

If you properly PREP yourself, you can carry on meaningful and insightful conversations with your colleagues, clients and others. More importantly, following these tips will allow you to state your opinions and reasons for doing certain activities so that everyone understands your motivations.

(8)

MTV & VH-1 are not enough!

OK – so your job is a "brain drain" and "chilling out" is all you want to do in your free time, but don't get too comfortable. Being a well-rounded professional requires information gathering. As we already covered earlier, the ability to make effective small talk is an essential part of the meeting and greeting process and overall networking know-how.

In order to be interesting, prepared to spot and seize opportunities and to move your career forward, you must be in touch with the rest of the world. Doing so may be easier and more stimulating than you think. Here's the plan:

- **Read at least one newspaper a day.** If you have limited time, pick up *USA Today,* sometimes affectionately referred to as "McPaper" because it's quick and easy to read. It is written – as many journalism professors would say writing should be – on a sixth-grade level. The paper gives you the basics to keep you informed and get involved in conversations.

  Whatever paper you choose, read the entire thing or at least skim the headlines on all pages and read one or two paragraphs of each article. If everyone in your department talks about a certain topic such as sports, it may be worthwhile for you to pay particular attention to that section as a way of becoming part of the group. If you have more time, also read a local newspaper.

- **Read at least one newsmagazine a week** (*BusinessWeek, Newsweek, Time,* etc.) that will keep you abreast of news and other happenings around the world.

- **Read magazines which are of interest to you,** but also consider expanding your horizons by including *Fortune, Inc., Business 2.0, Fast Company,* etc., along with magazines related to your field.

- **Read several best-seller books (business, fiction, biographies).** Not only will you learn something, you will be able to have better conversations with a variety of people. If you don't have time to read, get books on tape so you can listen when commuting or exercising.

- **Always read your company's publications** — newsletters, annual reports, Web pages, etc.

- **Read any information about the field and industry you're in.** This is available by joining associations and getting their materials and newsletters.

(9)

Be a lifelong learner

You may be a recent graduate – tired of exams, homework, etc., or think that studying is something from your distant past – but this isn't the time to stop your education. Individuals who continue to challenge themselves and learn new things demonstrate initiative and a special commitment to growth. Companies value lifelong learners. "Continuing education" can fall into many categories. They are:

- **Advanced degrees:** If it would help you to learn, stand out, acquire new knowledge, go ahead and get your MBA, M.A., M.S., Ph.D., etc. Many companies will even help you do this by subsidizing the tuition and giving you time off to take classes. If a company feels this strongly, isn't it worth *your* investment of time and money?

- **Certifications:** By joining professional organizations and fulfilling their requirements, you can become certified. Examples of certification include: CPA (Certified Public Accountant), CSP (Certified Speaking Professional), CMC (Certified Management Consultant) and CMP (Certified Meeting Professional). Check what might work for you in your field.

- **CEU credits:** In many professions, it is a requirement to take courses that will get you Continuing Education Units (CEUs) each year. The goal is to keep you current in your field.

- **Company training programs:** Many larger companies have training departments offering numerous programs. Take advantage of these programs. Not only do they give you networking opportunities, but they also provide great information about how you can enhance your presentation skills, etiquette awareness, conflict management, computer skills, etc.

- **Adult courses:** These types of courses are often offered through local high schools, colleges, public seminars and on-line training. Education opportunities are all around you.

Continually update your skills and acquire new knowledge. Information and application of it is power. If your company doesn't offer training programs, ask to be sent to external programs so you will regularly enhance your current skill set.

Look at your job – what skills/experience do you need to do it better? Do you want to improve your ability to communicate? Manage? Present? Use PowerPoint© slides? Do an Excel© spreadsheet? It is up to you to get the education and training you need. Never be shortsighted by limiting yourself to what you need now. Think about what you will need to perform better in the next one to five years.

(10)

I'm too sexy for this job

"The talent of success is nothing more than doing what you can do well, and doing well whatever you do." – Henry Wadsworth Longfellow

Want to know the secret formula for moving up in a company and for being given new opportunities, increased responsibility and higher compensation? Do your present job to the very best of your ability!

If you are a customer service representative, commit to being the best customer service rep your company has. If you are a sales consultant, be the most knowledgeable, skilled and innovative person in your district or region.

Too often, ambitious people spend more time wishing for or thinking about advancement than they do about the challenges at hand.

Here are some of the most common mistakes that prevent people from being considered for promotions or increased responsibilities:

- being unable to get along with others … difficult to work with.

- having a myopic view of their roles in the company. They get so bogged down in their own tasks that they lose sight of the big picture.

- failing to treat others with respect, regardless of title.
- spreading rumors or failing to maintain confidentiality.
- not paying attention to detail.
- not following through on commitments.

Come to work each day prepared to excel at your current position and be mindful of the list above. Your odds for growth and recognition will increase.

CLM Flash: "A person who enjoys responsibility usually gets it. A person who merely likes exercising authority usually loses it." – Malcolm Forbes

(11)

Command performance

Many companies sponsor parties and events. Even though you might prefer not to go, it is a good idea to attend. Many relationships are made in business/social situations because co-workers can get to know each other in less stressful environments.

If you keep these points in mind, you will feel more comfortable at these "command performances":

- R.S.V.P. – Respond to invitations.

- Arrive on time.

- Mingle with people – don't hang out only with your friends.

- Limit alcohol (one or two drinks maximum).

- Don't discuss work.

- Don't be the last to leave, but stay at least one hour.

- Don't pig out – this isn't about the food.

- Be on your best behavior – this is an office function.

- Thank the sponsor or host before leaving.

- Write a thank-you note.

- If this is in someone's honor, contribute money to a group gift or bring a gift.

You are judged by the company you keep. If you bring a guest, date or spouse, his or her behavior and appearance will directly reflect on you. Help this person to be appropriately prepared as well.

(12)

The "write" stuff

Even the most seasoned business professionals can suddenly become nervous when told they should write a report or proposal. Sometimes even writing a letter becomes a chore.

Don't worry. Becoming an effective business writer does not require a journalism degree. You first need to understand that different types of business writing exist, and they have their own styles and formats.

There are seven points to remember for any type of writing:

- **Be concise, not wordy.** Get right to the point.

- **Remember your audience.** Your writing should be geared to readers. Don't use words they won't know.

- **Keep it simple.** Having an impressive vocabulary is one thing, using stuffy words when writing is simply pretentious. Don't say "transpire" when you mean "happen."

- **Always check for spelling mistakes and grammar errors.** Even after you use a computer spell checker, do it the old fashioned way – with a dictionary and stylebook. The computer has limitations.

- **Before a final draft is mailed or sent, print a hard copy.** Read this carefully; many mistakes are found even at this stage.

- **Have someone else read it.** The writer is always too close to the work to remain objective.

- **Be active, not passive.** Never start a sentence with a passive phrase; it seems weak. Instead of "Since sales have increased, the firm can offer a bonus" use "The firm can offer a bonus since sales have increased."

Memos, Letters, Proposals, Etc.

Memos – by their very definition, memos should be brief. If your comments can't fit on one page, write a letter. Memos are best written with the following elements:

DATE: Day, month and year (needed because people file memos).

TO: The main person(s) receiving the memo.

CC: This used to mean "Carbon Copied." List other people who will be receiving the memo.

FYI: People listed in the "for your information" space do not need to respond to the memo. Perhaps a name here could be your assistant, who may file all memos you send.

FROM: Your full name and title (add company name if recipient is outside the firm).

RE (or SUBJECT): Keep this as short as possible, and put it in boldface for emphasis.

Letters – should be direct and easily understood. You can use a more conversational style in letters than in proposals. Contractions, for example, are OK to use sparingly in letters. Unless they're personal, a thank-you note, or informal, all letters should be done on a computer or typewriter – especially sales letters. All letters should contain the following elements:

DATE: Day, month and year.

RECIPIENT NAME: Use the person's full name with Mr. or Ms. (Unless the woman prefers Mrs.), Dr. (doctor), Rev. (Reverend), etc. Always check to ensure the person's name is spelled correctly. One spelling mistake can cost you a client.

JOB TITLE: If you know it, use it.

ADDRESS: Don't forget suite numbers or floors.

SALUTATION: Always use a person's name, never "To Whom It May Concern" or "Dear Sir or Madam." If you don't know or can't get the name, consider using "Good morning!" instead.

BODY OF LETTER: Include actions that need to be taken, information you want to relay.

SIGNATURE: Use your full name with title underneath. Signing only a first name is more informal, and is acceptable if you know the recipient well enough to begin your letter with "Dear Joe" vs. "Dear Mr. Smith." You can sign in a different color ink for emphasis (if the letter is typed in black, then sign in blue or green, etc.).

MISCELLANEOUS: At the bottom of the letter, put "Enclosures" (or "Enc.") if you are enclosing additional documents; if you are sending copies of the letter to another person, write "CC:" followed by the person's name.

Proposals – Writing formal proposals doesn't have to be troublesome. Proposals that are easy to understand and personalized get attention. Consider these four suggestions:

- **Remember that a book is often judged by its cover.** Put the prospective client's company name and logo (if possible), and the name of the person reviewing it at the top of the proposal as a header.

- **Pictures often speak louder than words.** Blend pictures or other graphics (charts, etc.) with your words to make the proposal more appealing and exciting.

- **Bullets and boldface work.** Make the proposal easy to read by using bullets with lists and boldface type for headings.

- **Write an index** if the proposal is long.

News Releases & Other Promotional Writing – Approach promotional writing in an entirely different way from other forms of business writing. The primary goal of advertising copy should be to position the product, service or company. Be concise and clear. Every now and then you can use an exclamation point for emphasis, but don't over do it.

Oh, Behave!

(1)

Life in the land of prairie dogs

Dilbert certainly has pointed out the difficulties of working in a cubicle. His cartoons depict this reality for thousands in the business world as a life akin to prairie dogs – with professionals jutting their heads from time to time to view the lay of the land.

Comic strips aside, it is important to learn how to manage cubicle life long enough to work your way to the corner office.

Personalize your cubicle with a plant or pictures. Keep it neat and organized so you can find things easily.

Rules to remember:

- Keep your voice low whether you are on the phone or with others.

- Knock before entering.

- If the person is on the phone or deep in thought, go away and come back or call later.

- Never "borrow" anyone's supplies or other possessions, even if the items are visible on a desk, unless you ask permission first.

What's with this barging into people's space? Do you like it when you are in the middle of a great thought and are rudely interrupted by an uninvited visitor? Even though most people live in a world of cubicles (a "no-door society"), it is still disrespectful to barge in. So, what to do? Knock on the cube wall – or door if it is an office – and ask if this is a good time to talk. Don't hover when others are on the telephone. Don't look over someone's shoulder to see what he or she is working on.

CLM Flash: According to ZDNet.com, it's just plain rude for cubicle dwellers to listen to Web radio, streaming audio or other multimedia without headphones. The same is true of keeping any "alert" chimes and sounds turned up so everyone around you can hear each time your system pings to notify you of instant messaging, new e-mails and mistakes.

(2)

Don't put your elbows on the table!

That's one of the first things people think of when asked for some table-manner advice. But, it's only the beginning of etiquette rules concerning business dining.

It doesn't matter if you are eating at the company cafeteria or at an elegant restaurant, proper dining etiquette *does* matter, whether you are a guest or the host.

Knowing and practicing the following guidelines may prevent you from getting a bad case of indigestion and embarrassment. Here are 10 tips:

- **Pass food, don't reach.**
- **Chew with your mouth closed.** Wait until you've swallowed your food before speaking.
- **Be pleasant.** Don't complain about the food or criticize the service. The host can leave the table and deal with bad service. Guests should say nothing.

- **Know your silverware.** Use utensils that are on the outside first and work your way in.

- **Know what is yours.** Your food (bread and butter plate and salad plate) is to your left – your drinks are to the right.

- **Be thoughtful about smoking.** If you smoke, don't assume that your guest or host won't mind sitting in the "smoking section." Some people have allergies or simply find cigarette smoke offensive while eating. As a considerate host, you should refrain from smoking unless your guest smokes. As a polite guest, you should ask your host's permission before lighting up. You can say something like, "Would you mind if I smoke? If so, don't worry, I can wait until later." It is never appropriate to smoke during a meal. Wait until everyone has finished eating. Best bet – don't smoke.

- **Pass the salt and pepper together** even if only one of the two is requested.

- **Don't put your elbows on the table or wave utensils around.**

- **Bring food to your mouth,** not your mouth to the food.

- **Know your napkin placement.** When you are finished eating, the napkin goes on the table to the left of the plate.

You can truly demonstrate your social manners, and save the day, by making your guest feel welcome at the table – even if he or she makes an etiquette gaffe.

(3)

May I take your order?

We already briefly touched on table manners. But, since the business meal is one of the most commonly mishandled situations in one's professional life, it is worth a closer look – so *you* don't get egg on your face.

An executive recruiter we know makes it a policy to take any individual he is seriously considering as a candidate out for a meal. Sometimes it's in an upscale restaurant, other times it might be in a company dining room or more casual setting. Why does he do this? There are many reasons. He, like many others, believes that table manners say a lot about an individual. Is the candidate thoughtful and considerate not only of his or her dining companion, but of others such as the server, hostess and other diners? Does the candidate eat off the correct bread plate, know what to do with his or her napkin and use the right eating utensils? Is the candidate nitpicky about the service or food?

In today's increasingly relaxed and casual business environment, you may try to convince yourself that dining protocol is obsolete and no longer relevant. Living with that false assumption could cost you a lot more than a fancy five-course meal.

Help! Was That a Career Limiting Move?

Here are some rules to make you feel comfortable and keep you from having an unnecessary case of indigestion:

Ordering at a restaurant

- If you are the host, make recommendations to the guest.

- Let your guest order first.

- Order in the same price range as your guest.

General behavior

- Don't discuss business topics until the order has been taken (unless your guest mentions something).

- Treat the server with dignity and respect.

- Know how to use your silverware.

- Chew with your mouth closed and don't talk while chewing food.

- Put your napkin on your lap when everyone is seated. If you leave the table during the meal for any reason, the napkin goes on the seat of your chair. At the end of the meal, it goes to the left of your plate.

- Don't wave your silverware around when talking.

- At a cafeteria or buffet-style restaurant, clean up after yourself.

- Don't do any personal grooming at the table (applying lipstick, using a comb, flossing teeth, using toothpicks, blowing nose, etc.). Excuse yourself from the table if you need to do any of these activities. If you can't prevent from using a tissue or handkerchief at the table (a sneeze suddenly gets the best of you, you have seasonal allergies, etc.), turn away from the table and say "excuse me" once you are finished. Remember, don't use your napkin to blow your nose.

- Break your bread one piece at a time before buttering it.

- Taste the food before adding salt or pepper.

- Don't cut all of your food at one time, like you did when you were 5 years old.

- When out with clients and colleagues, don't ask for a "doggie bag."

Tips

- When service is acceptable, it is expected that you leave a 15% tip at minimum – usually on top of tax. If the service is exceptional, the tip could be up to 20% of the bill.

- If you are a guest, write a thank-you note to the host or hostess.

A considerate, well-mannered diner is usually a considerate, well-mannered employee.

(4)

After you. No, after *you*!

Exactly who *does* go through the door first? It used to be that a man always would hold the door open for a woman. That is no longer the case in our gender-equal workplace. If a man holds the door open for a woman, she should accept graciously. Women should not, however, *expect* this to happen in our increasingly gender-blind business world.

The rules of the game have changed and it's important to know what they are:

- Whoever gets to the door first can go through (regardless of gender) or … let the person with most seniority go first.

- If you get to the door first, open it and hold it for the person or people you are walking with. Never walk through a door and let it slam in someone's face.

- If you are waiting for an elevator, bus, train, etc., stand to the side instead of in front of the door to let others get off easily.

- It is not necessary for women to get off an elevator first. Whoever is closest to the door, gets off. If the elevator is crowded, stand to the side, or get off to let others exit, then get back on to continue to your floor.

- At revolving doors, if you are the host, go through first, so you can lead the way. Push the door and greet your guest on the other side.

- When anyone takes the time to hold the door for you, always be gracious and thank the person. Don't just assume that he or she is your personal doorman.

(5)

It's all in the cards

Business cards can be traced back to the late 1600s, when slightly larger versions were first used by skilled tradesmen of the upper class to provide information about a proprietor's location and wares.

The term "business card" was coined around 1880. Today's business card is your "stand-in when you aren't present – the handshake you leave behind," according to *The Business Card Book* by Dr. Lynella Grant.

In some countries, the exchange of business cards is governed by time-honored rituals. But in the United States, the circumstances, timing and presentation of cards is not quite as formal. In this country, business cards are traditionally exchanged either at the beginning or end of the first encounter.

If you want to offer your card, ask for the other person's card first. In most cases, the other person will then ask for yours. If not, offer it. This is much more gracious than thrusting your card at him or her. If the other person doesn't have a business card, but you want his or her contact information, take your card, cross off the front and get the details on the back. This way you won't accidentally give out this person's information when distributing your own cards.

There are times and places when handing out business cards is not good etiquette. For example, it is not appropriate to distribute cards during a meal. If you want to initiate a card exchange, wait until everyone is finished eating. If you are at a private dinner party, you may bring your cards with you, but don't give out any unless someone specifically asks you for one.

Above all, make sure your business cards suit your professional image. They should be well-designed and printed on high-quality paper. They should be free of wrinkles, smudges and tattered edges.

Never interrupt a conversation to exchange business cards and don't distribute your card in batches. Take the time to hand them out individually, giving the receiver the proper attention.

If your company doesn't give you business cards, consider making them on your own computer and printer. There are many software programs that have business card templates. Special perforated paper stock also makes this process easy. Your card can include your name, phone number, address and any Internet addresses (e-mail and Web site, if applicable), or just print your name and handwrite the information you want to give to the person who is receiving the card.

Having a homemade business card or calling card sure beats ripping a napkin and writing your information on that! If you make your own card because your company doesn't give you one, don't put company information on the card – keep it personal.

CLM Flash: The word "aptronym" (coined by Franklin P. Adams) relates to a person whose business card likely would cause double takes – if the name on the card is aptly suited for the person's profession, such as a judge named Jessica Justice. Although often amusing, be sensitive to the person who bears this type of name. He or she will undoubtedly have heard comments in the past, which may either be offensive or trite.

(6)

What's in a name? Plenty!

When someone says, "I can't remember names," the first thing we think is that the person is really egocentric. Most people don't remember names because they don't really try and they certainly aren't concentrating when a name is given. Remember, this isn't homecoming season when you meet tons of people while you're partying and can forget their names one hour later.

When being introduced, LISTEN, FOCUS, CONCENTRATE! Pretend everyone is the CEO of the company, whose name you likely will remember. Be sure to look at the person's eyes (check out his or her eye color). That stops you from looking around the room. Repeat the name as soon as you hear it, "It's nice to meet you, _____." If you didn't get it the first time, immediately ask, "Please tell me your name again." Then repeat it.

Listen carefully and use the name that is requested. It is not appropriate to use nicknames unless you are asked to do so. If someone is introduced or introduces herself as Sandra, don't say, "Nice to meet you, Sandy." However, some people named John like being called Jack. Do so if requested.

In the United States, we tend to use first names. Don't expect this informality to work with every business professional, in every country. Be alert to and respectful of differing cultures and protocols.

A safe bet, especially when you have any degree of uncertainty, is to ask, "What do you prefer to be called?"

(7)

"Graçias … merçi … thanks!"

Guess what? Annoying parental reminders may be a thing of the past, but the need to send thank-you notes will never go away!

Thank-you notes are a vital part of business and reinforce good working relationships. If a prospective client is pitched the same services in a sales meeting by two different companies and only one rep sends a thank-you note for the prospect's time, who do you think has a better chance of getting the business?

When you are interviewed for a new job or promotion, always take the time to send a thank-you note to those who interviewed you immediately following your time together. This gives you an opportunity to demonstrate proper business manners, show that you were a good listener and reiterate that you are the best candidate for the position.

Thank-you notes also should be written for nice things that people do for you, extra help, etc. They only need to be three to four sentences long and actually take very little time to write.

Help! Was That a Career Limiting Move?

First, find out if your company has note paper or cards. If it doesn't, get your own. The paper should be good quality, usually white or cream colored. Either the company name or your name can be printed on it. Don't have "thank you" already printed on the paper, that way you can use it for a variety of reasons.

Don't type your thank-you notes. Penning them by hand adds a more personal touch. If you want to go that extra step, use a fountain pen – that's classy!

It's OK to send some thank-you messages via e-mails – especially if that's how you do most of your corresponding with the person, or if you don't have any other contact information. But, by taking your time to send a handwritten note, you will be remembered in a more positive way.

Bottom line is send them! And, send thank-you notes in a timely fashion – soon (no more than 48 hours) after the action or service that you are recognizing was completed.

Once, after an annual team meeting at a large company, we asked the individual who put together the whole affair if she got any thank-you notes. She said two – one from the managing director, one from the senior vice president. How is it that they were the only two people to take the time to acknowledge the work that was done?

In our business travels, we repeatedly see that the people in key leadership and senior positions within companies are far more likely to be those who consistently do the seemingly "little things" that often make a big difference.

(8)

Parlez vous, "Sorry, I can't make it?"

If you retain only one thing from French 101, remember the importance of R.S.V.P., which stands for *"Répondez, s'il vous plaît."* It means "Please reply."

If someone has been thoughtful or kind enough to invite you to a special event or celebration, it is only reasonable to expect that you will let him or her know whether you are able to attend.

Just imagine that you are having a party, serving food and drinks. You invite 50 people – 10 tell you they are coming. Now you order food, drinks, etc., for 10, and all 50 show. You will have a lot of hungry, thirsty, complaining people. Sometimes people say they are coming, and don't show. This means the host has paid for a lot of extra food and drinks that may go to waste.

Bottom line – not responding to an invitation is rude. Be courteous enough to respond – one way or the other. Do so by the date requested so that the host is not burdened by the additional work of seeking you out to get your answer. Then, show up when you say you will.

(9)

Rude and crude

It just amazes us what people say. We can only assume that the individuals who spew expletives and insults would be shocked to realize that they are committing career suicide. Here are some language "no-nos":

Don't ...

- use foul language. You know what they are – the ones that get "bleeped" on the radio and TV, and don't appear in the daily newspaper. These words are inappropriate everywhere, but particularly in a work environment. Many people find such language offensive. Others think it shows a limited vocabulary. What if a client calling in overhears one choice expletive?

- be sarcastic. Putting people down, or being snide isn't funny – it's painful.

- gossip. It's one thing to know what is going on around you, it's another to spread rumors. If others come to you with gossip, run. Don't be associated with them.

- use pretentious language. Speak words that the people you work with understand. Your goal is to connect, not impress and make them feel stupid.

- use jargon, buzzwords and acronyms – unless *everyone* understands them. This is too exclusive, making others feel left out.

- tell dirty, racist, sexist, religious or ethnic jokes. These will offend many people and make you look ignorant. And, in today's litigious society, they could even translate into a lawsuit!

- make fun of anyone. 'Nuff said.

CLM Flash: A survey by The Sunday Times (England) found that 70% of 400 readers questioned thought society is ruder now than it was five years ago, while 42% thought rudeness was necessary "to get your own way." Want to be set apart and recognized as being above average? Try being kind.

(10)

That's mine

We continue to be surprised by the number of stories we hear about individuals who don't draw the line between what is theirs and what isn't.

People interested in new positions sometimes send résumés and personal correspondence printed on their current employer's letterhead or company envelopes. Our thought: The individual has some nerve using his or her present employer's property to gain new employment. No thanks!

Supplies and other items that belong to the company or a co-worker aren't community property. If you take them, it's stealing. Plain and simple. You didn't pay for the items, so they don't belong to you.

We're not talking about leaving work and panicking because you left a paper clip in your pocket, or a rubber band around your wrist. Here is a short list of things many people think they can take advantage of or use for personal reasons. Depending on your place of employment, you might add others.

- paper
- stamps

- copier machine
- Internet
- food that belongs to others
- pens, pencils, etc.
- things from other people's desks (calendars, clocks, etc.)
- making long-distance phone calls

Respect others' property and belongings as you hope they would yours. When in doubt, ask.

(11)

Make the most of meetings

When you're invited to attend a meeting, remember the "3 P's": *preparation, punctuality and participation.*

- **Preparation.** Ask the person planning the meeting what is expected of you. What will be your role during the meeting? What materials or information should you bring?

- **Punctuality.** Arrive on time. Whether you're meeting with one person or 10, making people wait is bad manners and bad for your image.

- **Participation.** Present your materials and ideas. Keep your comments brief and to the point. Stick to the agenda. Listen with an open mind to what others have to say. Ask questions when you need something to be clarified. Make notes on any follow-up actions you will be expected to take.

After the meeting, review the minutes and brief anyone in your department who should be aware of the results and the follow-up actions. Complete your follow-up actions on or before the deadline.

Things NOT to do during a meeting:

✓ conduct sidebar conversations when someone else has the "floor"

✓ put down others

✓ do a crossword puzzle or other non-meeting-related work

✓ talk on a cell phone

✓ leave a beeper on (unless it's on "vibrate" mode)

✓ get your e-mail

✓ read a newspaper, magazine or other printed matter not related to the meeting

✓ do other work

Make sure the time is well-spent. Meetings are a way of life in most companies. When the time is well-spent, they can be very productive. If not, they can be a colossal waste. So, be prepared for meetings.

Here are some ways you can make meetings more valuable – even if you are only a participant and not the leader.

- When the agenda arrives, study it: Who is coming? Should others be there? Why are you invited?

- What are the meeting objectives? Ask yourself this question, "How do I need to prepare in order to participate?"

- If there are no objectives or agenda, you could contact the leader and say: "I want to be prepared for the meeting. Is there an agenda? What are the objectives?"

- Make sure you arrive on time or early. Come with any materials you might need, including a pen and pad of paper.

- Listen and participate. Generally speaking, if you don't participate within the first 10 minutes, you become a non-entity.

- Watch your body language at meetings

  ✓ Sit up.

  ✓ Don't doodle.

  ✓ Don't fidget or tap your feet.

  ✓ Avoid pointing your finger or making a fist.

(12)

Planes, trains and opportunities

Unless you walk to work, or drive your own car, you most likely are taking public transportation: train, bus, monorail, van, boat, plane or taxi. Regardless of what type of transportation you use, there is a code of behavior that you should follow.

There are two reasons to pay attention to the following list. First, because it is important to behave in a decent, respectful and considerate way. Second, networking opportunities often present themselves in the way of serendipitous encounters.

The code looks like this:

- Don't jump ahead of others in line.

- Don't carry so much "stuff" that you are bumping others and taking their space.

- Keep the volume of your voice down.

- Avoid pushing and shoving.

- Limit – or better yet, eliminate – cell phone use.

- Have money and tickets ready so you don't hold up lines.

- Don't litter.

- Don't take more than one seat.

- Don't eat or drink on vehicles.

- "No smoking" means just that – don't smoke!

- Even if you're using headphones, no one else should hear what's on your personal radio/music player – so keep the volume down.

- Don't overdose on hairspray, perfume or cologne. Some people have sensitive noses or allergies to such "heavy" smells.

- Don't do any personal grooming (shaving, putting on makeup, etc.) in any public vehicle.

Adhering to the code will make you a respectable passenger. Sadly enough, this kind of good behavior is not necessarily the norm. Other properly mannered and considerate passengers may recognize you as someone who shares their sense of courtesy when they encounter boorish passengers. This may pave the way for networking (sharing a common experience). Have your business card, proper introduction and a good handshake ready to seize the opportunity.

(13)

A touchy subject

Office romance has been the stuff of great movies as well as searing scandals. There are those who see it as an inevitable part of life. Let's face it -- most of us spend more of our waking hours with co-workers than we do with family and friends. On the flip side, like the saying went in World War II, "loose lips sink ships." We've also seen that loose lips can sink careers and companies.

So what's a person to do? First and foremost, be mindful of the fact that when and if unexpected romantic feelings develop, you need to ensure that acting on them does not compromise the integrity of your position or company in any way. How do you know? Ask yourself these questions:

- Is this someone who I report to or who reports to me? If the answer is "Yes," then there could be an issue. This type of business relationship requires fair, consistent and impartial judgment about such things as performance and compensation. Being personally involved (no matter what you might think) can prevent that from happening.

- Do the two of you work in different departments that have been created as a check and balance for the company? For example, is one of you in production and the other in quality assurance? If so, your relationship could compromise that process.

- Is one of you in a senior level position that requires a significant amount of confidentiality about company finances, proprietary products or human resource issues? Being personally involved with a more junior employee could lead to speculation about numerous sensitive issues and bring unwelcome scrutiny.

- Are you in the same department or work on the same team, and if so, how will your work and co-workers be affected by this new level of familiarity between the two of you? More importantly still, what if the romance turns sour? How will that affect your ability to stay focused and do your job well while personal feelings may be overwhelming you?

It is easy to rationalize away or dismiss the situations noted above -- especially when love is in the air. However, it is very shortsighted to do so. Think all of this through before you make that first date or find yourself in the arms of Mary or John in the cubicle next door.

All that said, if you do take that step from professional acquaintance to "love of my life" and you're not violating any company policies or standards that we've discussed, be mindful that discretion and respect for others is critical.

Finally, the issue of sexual harassment in the workplace is one that is taken very seriously. Employers have a responsibility to ensure that all employees work in an environment free from this situation. If anyone makes comments or gestures of a personal or sexual nature that make you uncomfortable, report it to your manager or human resource department immediately.

Help! Was That a Career Limiting Move?

Professional Presence

(1)

Breaking out clean

Going to work requires more than rolling out of bed and throwing on your clothes. Sure, it worked when you were in college for those early morning classes, but in the business world, *everyone* must pay attention to personal grooming or risk being perceived as lazy, disorganized or indifferent. Check out this list. How do *you* rate?

<u>The well-groomed ...</u>

- keep their hair trimmed, clean and dandruff-free.

- men shave daily or have a well-kept mustache or beard.

- women get rid of facial hair through waxing, electrolysis or shaving.

- men eliminate any exposed nose or ear hairs.

- keep nails clean and trimmed and don't bite them. Women who use nail polish – don't let it chip.

- have clean, white teeth. Today, with the advent of teeth whiteners, braces for adults and good dentistry, there is little reason to walk around with poor oral hygiene.

- carry dental floss. This allows people to check to see if there is anything stuck in their teeth and take care of it. They know that they won't be taken seriously if they have a piece of Tootsie Roll® or spinach in their teeth.

- don't look like a Barbie® doll. Too much makeup often gives the impression that you aren't serious. On the other hand, most women look better with a little makeup – it's a more finished look.

- don't have bad hair days, weeks or months. What "worked" in school may no longer "cut it" – especially for conservative companies' cultures or customers.

- bathe and shower regularly. Body odors are offensive and people talk, so don't wear too much cologne or perfume. A good guideline is if people compliment you about your perfume in the afternoon, you were probably wearing too much in the morning. Other sources of offensive odors include: smoking, sweat, bad breath and dirty hair. Remember, if you eat spicy or garlic-filled foods, the odor often comes through your pores when you sweat. Use mouthwash and mints as a way to ensure your breath is approachable.

- clean their ears. Ear wax can really gross out your co-workers.

- make sure that their appearance never becomes an obstacle or distraction from the talent and contributions they bring to their companies.

How often have you chosen something based on its packaging? It is your responsibility to ensure that your appearance reflects the level of pride and care you take in *your* package.

(2)

Read my lips … and other rules of good body language

We've all heard the expression, "Actions speak louder than words." And it's certainly true, especially when it comes to your body language.

Without even saying a word, a person can convey confidence or arrogance, interest or apathy, openness or hostility through body language.

Here are some pointers to enhance what your body language is saying about you:

- Stand straight, keep feet still and shoulders relaxed.

- Move purposefully and have a deliberate stride. Bend from the knees when picking up objects.

- Use gestures to enhance, not distract, by keeping your arms open and your movements smooth and embracing. Avoid finger pointing, fist raising and crossing your arms in front of you or holding them behind you (the "military parade rest" stance).

- Smile and make direct eye contact. Don't frown, stare or have shifty eyes.

Make sure that you are not guilty of some of the most common distracting behaviors. Be sure not to:

- tug or play with your hair or comb it in public.
- play with, pick or bite fingernails.
- tap feet.
- fidget.
- scratch/pick nose.
- pick teeth.
- put on makeup or nail polish in public.
- crowd people's space.

The goal is to let your body language add credibility and interest to what you are saying or doing. Good body language prevents people from mentally shutting the door before you open your mouth.

(3)

Oral fixation

If you want people to pay attention to what you have to say, not to your mouth …

<u>Don't …</u>

- chew gum in the workplace. You can look like a cow and sound even worse. You can crack it, which is most annoying, and you could forget and blow bubbles. It's best to wait until you are home or in the car before popping in a piece of gum.

- smoke. The smell drives people crazy. You are forced to go outside and rarely will it be senior executives that you are hanging out with. It is also expensive, plus your clothes need to be cleaned more frequently – not to mention you might live longer.

- pick your teeth – with toothpicks, fingertips or anything else in public. If you get something stuck in your teeth, go to the restroom and use dental floss. Sometimes, when there is no floss, a business card can work well, too. But again, be discreet!

- chew with your mouth open. It is gross. Close your mouth when chewing and everyone around you will be happy.

- bite your fingernails. It is a nasty habit and makes you look unprofessional.

- eat while you're on the phone or when meeting someone face to face. Eating candy, etc., is fine, just not while you are talking in person or on the phone. Swallow or spit it out before using the telephone!

CLM Flash: In a posting to an Internet News Group about pet peeves, one professional female related this about gum chewing: "I recently watched two well-paid telemarketers lose their jobs due to their refusal to not chew gum while serving customers on the phone. I also watched a young lady walk into a job interview chewing gum and then wonder why she didn't get the job. Several teachers tell me this behavior is one of the primary problems they have in classrooms." Our advice: Don't let chewing gum get you in a sticky situation!

(4)

All dressed up and no place to go

Jim was interviewing for a job, and things seemed to be going pretty well until the hiring manager asked Jim if he had any questions. "Just one," said Jim. "Which days are dress-down days?" The hiring manager looked disappointed and replied, "Saturday and Sunday."

Dressing for work can be tricky. It's easy when you wear a uniform, but most people don't. It's difficult to define appropriate business wardrobe, because it really depends on the type of job you have, the industry you're in, the part of the country (or world) you are in, and the company culture.

Check out any dress codes before joining a firm. Look at your managers – how are they dressed? It is important to understand the culture of your company and go with the office norm. The goal is to have your performance and contributions stand out -- not what your're wearing.

There is a difference between business professional, business casual and dress down. Dress down is never acccptable in a business environment. Here are a few guidelines about each:

Business Professional

The following items are acceptable as business attire for women:
- Suit – black, gray, dark burgundy or navy
- Contrasting jacket and skirt
- Two-piece dress
- White or off-white blouse
- Solid color blouse (may be pastel)
- Gold or silver earrings
- Scarf that picks up colors from the suit
- Black, navy or taupe pumps
- Neutral or taupe hosiery
- Black, dark brown or burgundy leather handbag
- All-weather coat
- Black, brown or burgundy briefcase

"Business professional" wardrobe options for men are:

- Suits – solid-color navy, gray and charcoal gray (one each color)
- Black socks, two pairs navy socks
- Pin-striped navy suit, same in gray
- Ties – burgundy, red print, navy, mauve, striped silk and patterned silk
- Navy sport coat with gray trousers
- Black leather belt
- White cotton shirts, a blue or pin-striped shirt
- Black leather briefcase
- Black slip-on shoes, or black lace-up shoes

Business Casual

Women have the following options for "business casual":

- Skirts and slacks
- Neatly pressed chinos or corduroys
- Cotton shirts in solids, prints or muted plaids
- Sweaters (not too tight)
- Blazers (structured and non-structured)
- Low-heeled shoes or boots with stockings or socks

Men can wear the following as acceptable "business casual":

- Slacks, Chinos or "Dockers"-type trousers
- Sport shirts with collars or banded necks
- Polo shirts (with collars)
- Sweater or sport jacket
- Casual loafers or lace-up shoes (with socks)

Dress Down & Weekend Wear (never acceptable in a corporate environment)

- Leggings
- T-shirts
- Bare midriffs
- Low-cut garments, front or back
- Hats, caps
- Ripped or tattered clothing
- Extremely tight-fitting blouses, short skirts or other suggestive clothing

- Jeans (depending on your business environment)
- Shorts

CLM Flash: Sloppy dressers are crossing the line, according to 34% of the 3,500 executives polled by Management Recruiters International. These executives mention tank tops, sweatshirts and open-toed shoes in the workplace as examples of "weekend casual" and inappropriate in any office setting.

(5)

Keep your clothes from making you look all washed up

Your clothes should be in good shape. Don't be one of those people who throw their clothes on the floor or on a chair, and then pick them up in the morning and wear them again. The clothes will look like you slept in them, which could damage the professional impressions you make.

It's not enough to have good personal hygiene. You also need to have a wardrobe that is well-maintained and appropriate.

Remember to …

- have clothes dry-cleaned or washed regularly.

- have clothes pressed.

- ensure that no buttons are missing and that there are no holes, tears or rips. It's hard to take someone seriously whose pants are held together by a safety pin.

- have all clothes properly hemmed.

- have clothes that fit. Look at yourself in the mirror – front and back. If the clothes are too tight, change. If they are too loose, change. Get your clothes altered to fit your current body – this includes sleeve length, which must be at your wrist, not in the middle of your hand or at your elbow.

Make sure that …

- shoes are polished and in good shape – no worn-down heels.

- stockings don't have runs (bring extra pairs for backup).

- socks go over the calf.

- ties (if you wear them) hit the top or middle of your belt.

Dress in a manner consistent with the rising stars and most respected people in your company. The workplace is not where you should attempt to "find yourself" with daring fashion choices.

(6)

Like nails on a blackboard

Despite what technology has done for us in the way of often reducing the need for human interaction in the workplace, daily exposure to -- and collaboration with -- a wide variety of people is never going away.

That said, we decided to compile our own unabridged list of business behaviors that we hear and see drives colleagues and customers alike simply batty.

So we asked, and we listened to complaints about the sort of things that make people cringe. Everyone we spoke with had one or two pet peeves.

Some things on this list are also noted in other sections of the book. We believe that in these cases, repetition is a good thing. You can't be reminded too often to stop doing those things that are making people around you crazy, while possibly tarnishing, if not ruining your reputation.

Here they are in no particular order ... remind you of anyone?

Help! Was That a Career Limiting Move?

- Chomping food, slurping your beverage, and letting the person dining with you see the contents of your mouth and the unwanted view of what your meal might look like if run through a Cuisinart.

- Blowing your nose so loudly that the person in the next cubicle mistakes the sound to be an air siren.

- If you're a man using a co-ed bathroom -- leaving the toilet seat up.

- Clipping your nails in a meeting, in your cubicle, in the lunchroom -- anywhere someone can hear you or be a victim of the resulting flying particles.

- Growing your nails so long that your ability to type, make phone calls, etc., is seriously diminished -- resulting in the person you are supposed to be assisting cringing with every missed key and click that you make.

- Saying, "Hey, that's not my job."

- Being habitually late and thinking that if you come up with a good enough excuse, it's acceptable. Worse still, thinking that your time is more important than anyone else's so everyone should understand.

- Leaving your cell phone on all the time and believing that if it rings -- even if you're with other people -- the caller is more important.

- Popping into a co-worker's office or workspace without notice or consideration for what the person might be doing to gripe, talk about your wild night, or make your newest priority or activity his or her priority -- without asking if it's a good time to do so.

- Picking your teeth.

- Leaving voice-mail messages that put the listener to sleep.

- Leaving your phone number on a message and gathering speed with each digit, until the last four numbers become totally inaudible for the poor person trying to listen, keep up with you and write them down.

- E-mailing co-workers when they sit 4 feet away.

- Asking someone to return your call and not leaving your phone number.

- Neglecting to make sure that you have fresh breath, no body odor and clean clothes.

- Sifting through the items in -- or on -- somebody's desk like you're an investigative reporter for "Entertainment Tonight."

- Yelling or swearing at your computer.

- Just throwing things on top of people's desks even though they have an "in-bin" or designated mail spot.

- Telling offensive jokes that directly make fun of someone because of their race, sex, religion, political beliefs, weight or hair color.

- Punishing your coworkers because you had a flat tire on the way to work, your boyfriend/girlfriend ditched you, your overbearing mother is making you go to Uncle Phil's 80th birthday party, your credit card has been "maxed" out or because you have a hangover from last night's celebration.

- Being so loud that nearby co-workers know more about your personal life and after-work activities than your next of kin.

(7)

Expect the unexpected

You know the Boy Scouts' motto, "Be prepared?" This philosophy is particularly relevant in the business environment.

Here are 15 reminders that may keep you from having a really bad day:

- Women – have an extra pair of stockings in case you get a run. Men – if you still wear a tie, keep a clean one available.

- Have dental floss or toothpicks for any food-in-teeth problems.

- Carry lots of quarters and $1 bills for tips, parking meters and vending machines.

- Carry a sewing kit in your briefcase for last-minute emergency repairs.

- Men – have a razor available to manage 5 o'clock shadow.

- Have breath mints on hand.

- Keep tape around – it is good as a lint remover or to hold up hems.

- Always carry your business card with you everywhere you go.

- Keep important phone numbers and extensions handy whenever you are away from the office. (Numbers of hotels, family members, people you are meeting with, etc.).

- When using equipment, bring extra bulbs, batteries, cords, etc.

- When using computer technology for a presentation, be prepared for a systems crash. Bring transparencies, handouts, etc.

- Bring more materials for meetings and presentations in case extra people are there.

- Carry a Swiss army knife – it's good for a bunch of things you may encounter in your day (opening bottles, cutting paper, etc.).

- Keep a sports jacket or blazer in your office in case you have to "dress up" your business casual look.

- Keep an extra dress shirt available in case you spill something on yours during the day.

Take a moment after reading this section. **Is your emergency kit in order and accessible for your average working day?**

The extra effort you spend on this will undoubtedly pay off at some point, not just in saved embarrassment and inconvenience, but in other substantial ways that may affect your job. The distraction potential of not being prepared can destroy a person's confidence, schedule and focus. Why take the chance?

(8)

That stinks!

Although we briefly touched on this topic before, it bears repeating. Some people have more sensitive noses than others, but everyone has the right to an odor-free workplace. Aside from the sensitivity to smell, many people have allergies or are asthmatic. Be considerate.

What to do:

- Limit or eliminate cologne or perfume.

- Stop smoking.

- Clean clothes regularly.

- Wear deodorant.

- Bathe, shower and wash your hair regularly – more than once a week!

- Avoid eating foods that smell: garlic, onions, tuna fish, milk and other dairy products, etc.

- Brush your teeth, use dental floss and mouthwash, see your dentist regularly.

- Keep your shoes on. If they don't fit, buy another pair that does!

You can't expect that someone will tell you if you have an odor problem, but you can watch for subtle signs from others. If someone steps back while you are speaking, you have either invaded the person's space or offended his or her sense of smell.

Clients have told us that it is more difficult to pay attention to, or listen carefully to, someone who exudes an offensive odor.

(9)

Don't go up in smoke

Yes, smoking can be a stinky and controversial subject. In addition to being a major health risk, it is also becoming socially unacceptable. Smoking cost the United States *$81.8 billion* in lost productivity from 1995-1999.

Smoking is an intrusion in the workplace. Bottom line, smoke is an offensive odor! The smell clings to clothes, breath and hair. People complain. You end up hanging outside – not typically with the business leaders.

According to a survey published in *The Wall Street Journal* of 140 of the United States' 1,000 largest companies, 85% of businesses insist on having a smoke-free workplace. And, even more telling – a Gallup poll shows that 94% of Americans, smokers and nonsmokers, believe companies should either ban smoking totally in the workplace or restrict it to separately ventilated areas. Smoking employees have 34% more absences from work, are 29% more likely to have industrial accidents and are 40% more likely to suffer occupational injuries.

Don't become part of these statistics! If you must – smoke at home after work. Better yet, come up with a plan to quit. Some companies even offer incentive plans or free smoking cessation programs for employees who need help kicking the habit. Ask a supervisor and consult your doctor.

CLM Flash: In California, where smoking is banned in almost all workplaces, a Gallup poll showed that 95% of nonsmokers and 69% of smokers think this policy is a positive thing.

(10)

What school you went?

In reality, there's nothing funny about poor grammar. The way you use – or abuse – the English language says a lot about you, whether you realize it or not.

Just like misspelled words and incorrect punctuation creates an image of someone who lacks polish and attention to detail, so does your use of grammar, diction and enunciation.

Try this grammar test. Which sentences are correct?

1) Sam and me are going to the movies.

2) Give the book to Amy and I.

3) The phone call was meant for Marjorie and me.

4) The National Speakers Association will hold it's annual meeting in January.

5) The American Society of Training & Development changed its membership policies this spring.

Help! Was That a Career Limiting Move?

The correct sentences are 3 and 5. Here are the grammatically correct versions of sentences 1, 2 and 4:

1) Sam and **I** are going to the movies.

2) Give the book to Amy and **me**.

4) The National Speakers Association will hold **its** annual meeting in January.

Grammar is also an issue when you speak – with enunciation and pronunciation. Here is a list of some of the most commonly mispronounced words:

<u>Right</u>	<u>Wrong</u>
congratulations	congradulations
asterisk	astericks
nuclear	nucleer
comfortable	comfterble
acumen	acooomen
etcetera	excetera
ask	ax
beautiful	beeuudiful
water	wadder
mine	myun
especially	expecially

Don't use regional or slang-type expressions like "youse" for "you," "gimme" for "give me," "ain't" for "are not" and "am not" or "it's not" and "irregardless" for "regardless."

CLM Flash: "Good grammar is a lot like deodorant … you don't notice it unless it's absent." — Ann Bloch

(11)

It's not easy to love a slob

There are numerous ways to make a mess at work, and many places that can easily get trashed. The key is to clean up after yourself so no one else will be affected.

Here are some common cleanup courtesies:

- **In the bathrooms:** Make sure to wipe the sinks so no one else gets water on themselves, wipe off the toilet seats if necessary, flush toilets and throw paper into the trash.

- **In the cafeteria:** Clean up your own silverware, plates, cups, etc. Leave the table in good shape for others when you are finished.

- **In the lunchroom:** If using a shared refrigerator, keep your food covered and labeled with your name or initials. Throw away leftovers every few days. Don't eat other people's food, no matter how hungry you are! Wipe off counters and tables. If you are the last to take coffee, clean out the pot or make more.

- **Everywhere:** Throw all trash (including what others left on the floor) into a trash bin.

- **Always leave a meeting room or office as neat, if not neater,** than you found it.

People who are sloppy at work quickly get labeled as inconsiderate, disorganized and "out of it." Do your part to keep your work environment neat so that people will spend more time focusing on your talents than on your dusty trail.

You're Wired

(1)

Get connected. Stay connected.

You don't have to be a software or hardware guru (unless that is your industry/profession), but, you add more value to your organization when you are technologically savvy. There used to be a time when you didn't have to know this sort of thing, but today – with most business dictated by technology – it is a survival skill.

How do you keep up with technology when it is changing by the nanosecond? First, you need to become educated on what equipment is used in your job and the basics about operating it. Also, learn the software that is used. This can be done by reading the manual, through trial and error, or by taking a training seminar.

Be open to and ready to attend training programs to stay current. It is also important and fun to experiment. The Internet and good computer magazines can keep you on top of trends and innovations.

One of the best ways we've found to get and stay connected is to ask for help from people we know who appreciate and enjoy technology the most. Not only are these individuals knowledgeable, but the passion and appreciation they have for what technology has to offer makes our learning fun.

CLM Flash: ZDNet.com did an informal survey of Web site visitors and asked if people thought the amount of "power rudeness" (technology-related manners) is increasing, decreasing or staying the same. A whopping 88% (1,294 visitors) said it is increasing, 10% (144 people) thought these manners are staying the same, and only 2% (26 Web surfers) thought it was decreasing.

(2)

What's the 411 on phone manners?

Rarely is there a job that doesn't involve spending some time on the phone – with a customer, vendor or prospect. The way you speak on the phone says a lot about you, those you associate with, and the company you work for. Here are nine guidelines to help you do it well:

- **Answer your own phone promptly**. Answer all calls within three rings.

- **Pay attention to your voice.** Even if you're having a bad day or are feeling stressed out, be conscious of sounding pleasant. No matter what you are doing or how hassled you feel, when you answer the telephone your voice and manners should immediately communicate your professionalism and readiness to be of service. Take a deep breath before you pick up the phone. Then smile. This may sound silly, but the smile on your face comes through in your voice. If you can't muster the appropriate enthusiasm necessary for proper phone presence, go home. Your anger or negativity will be transparent and antagonize, frustrate, upset or alienate the person on the other end. Put a mirror next to your phone and look at yourself as you speak. Practice your smile.

(3)

Is that your cell or my cell?

It's great to be wired, but when is enough enough? If your company has a policy about keeping cell phones off during the day, do it. If it doesn't have such a rule, turn the ringer down or put the phone on vibrate mode so it doesn't disturb your colleagues.

Abuse of the cell phone is rampant – everyone complains, yet most people still do the very things they complain about. If you follow these guidelines, at least people won't complain about you.

- Don't use cell phones where others can overhear your conversation or where it will disturb them: bathrooms (yes, it happens), elevators, theaters, churches, meetings, restaurants or cafeterias, public transportation, celebrations, movies, concerts, other public gatherings, etc. Turn cell phones off or put them on vibrate when you find yourself in any of these situations or locations.

- Don't give personal information during cell phone calls – particularly about your clients or company. Lines and signals often get crossed and strangers may overhear sensitive details.

- Don't call others on their cell phones unless they have asked you to.
- If you leave someone a message when calling from your cell phone, don't assume that they received it. Many people complain of getting partial or garbled messages from individuals who have called from cell phones.

Think of the cell phone as a way to keep you connected in case of an emergency or as a way to increase your efficiency in conducting business, not as an extension of your social life into the business world. Ask yourself before picking up your cell phone: "Is this call necessary? Will it increase my ability to serve my company and my customers? Is calling from my cell phone my only option or could this call wait until I am back at the office?"

CLM Flash: The French government has given theaters and movie cinemas the green light to install cell phone jamming equipment, with the provision that only emergency calls be allowed through.

(4)

Phone tag is NOT an Olympic sport

Ah voice mail … what would we do without it? In many ways, this messaging technology has been one of the greatest inventions of the late 20th Century. On the other hand, it can be -- and often is -- a huge, time-wasting and frustrating communication option that runs amuck.

Individuals in large organizations and those in outside sales positions frequently lament about having -- and often encountering -- full mailboxes, and the laborious chore of "Ugh, I have to clear my voice mail." Then there's the torture of the dreaded chatty colleague who uses this electronic medium to carry on about little or nothing, saying in five minutes what could have been said in 30 seconds or less.

For every wasted minute sending or listening to a pointless or inefficient voice-mail message, there are squandered opportunities for more client interaction, more creative thinking and more overall tangible contributions to the bottom line.

There is also the very real risk that if you get a bad voice-mail reputation, your comments and requests may be overlooked or sidelined on a regular basis. Just think about it: Your manager has three spare minutes to check voice mail, and yours is one of 15 that need to be addressed. If you are known as a rambler and weather commentator vs. a "get right down to business" communicator, what do you think your chances are that you will be listened to rather than skipped over? Not good.

So, starting today, you can boost your image and productivity by remembering these key points for being respected & thoughtful when recording your own voice-mail messages and leaving them for others.

- Speak clearly, slowly and deliberately -- especially when giving telephone numbers and names. Help with spelling if appropriate.

- Don't call from a cell phone unless absolutely necessary, and you are certain that the connection is solid. This prevents garbled messages, two-part messages and cut-offs.

- Do not repeat your message -- say it only once and clearly.

- Do not give running commentary about your day, the weather, etc.

- Only need-to-know information should be given. If the person is interested in knowing more, he or she can call you.

- Avoid "fluff" statements like, "Hi! How are you?"

- If making more than one point or imparting more than one key piece of information, list them as tightly as you can -- preferably no more than two to three points. Writing them out in bulleted form in advance may help keep you focused. Anything longer probably requires a live telephone conversation.

- Don't leave open-ended messages that require unnecessary return calls such as, "John, I have that figure you needed for your meeting." Unless there is some extenuating circumstance surrounding the confidentiality of the information, etc., just leave the details requested and be done with it.

- People aren't mind readers -- especially busy ones. So, put your message into context, and provide the right amount of information or background for your question/answer to easily make sense to the listener so he or she doesn't have to call you back for clarification.

- Try to know as much as you can about the voice-mail system, especially if it's your own. If date and time are automatically recorded, there is no need to repeat that information on your message. Conversely, if the system doesn't capture that data, then you may need to make note of it especially for time-sensitive matters.

If you've already fallen into bad voice-mail habits, or if you're new at this exchange, one of the best things you can do is play back your messages before sending them. As you listen, ask yourself, "Was this clear? Did it get to the point? Could I have sent it with less extraneous information?" And finally, "If I had to listen to me a dozen times a day, would I cringe or welcome it?"

You can make the difference between someone smiling or groaning when they hear that voice-mail message #23 is from you.

(5)

So many buttons, so many lights … now what?

Speakerphones can be a great way to bring a group of people together for a conversation. However, be sure to let the person (or people) on the other end of the line know when you're using the speakerphone and immediately announce who is present in the room. If someone enters the room during the conversation, inform whoever is on the telephone right away.

You should use your speakerphone for only two reasons: for a conference call and if you ask people for permission to put them on speakerphone while you look up some information. Other than these two reasons, it's rude and lazy to use the speakerphone feature.

Another "no-no" is putting your voice mail on speakerphone. This is annoying to others who can hear it throughout the hallway, and it could be embarrassing to the person who left the voice-mail message -- especially if it was sensitive in nature.

Voice mail can contribute to the efficiency and effectiveness of your communication, or it can lead to misunderstandings and frustration. Don't let the latter happen to you!

If you're leaving a message on someone's voice mail, you want to leave a good impression. Here are four pointers to remember.

1) **Keep the message brief. Prepare, so you don't ramble.**

2) **Speak slowly and enunciate clearly.**

3) **Give your name and phone number at the beginning and end of the message.**

4) **Listen to the message you leave and rerecord it if necessary.**

When you record an outgoing message to greet callers on your own voice-mail system, be courteous and cheerful. Provide your callers with accurate information for reaching you at another time or place, or give them an idea of when you'll return their calls. If you will be out for extended periods of time, provide that information on your voice-mail message so that people have realistic expectations of you.

(6)

Get the fax ... and the other stuff, too

Whether or not you are fortunate enough to have a personal assistant or secretary, learn to use and respect office equipment.

Know your office equipment etiquette ... basic manners when it comes to using the photocopier, fax machine, printer, etc. These points for equipment protocol fall under four main areas.

- **If it's empty, fill it.** The photocopier is out of toner and you just had to make one copy. You have been waiting for an important fax, but the machine is out of paper. It's frustrating, isn't it? Remember that feeling the next time you get near the end of the toner, or see that the fax paper tray or printer paper tray is empty. You don't have to be an electronic genius or spend a lot of time to reset/refill these machines. "I don't know how" is a lame excuse. Ask someone to help you. Learn.

- **If it's broken, fix it, or at least get it fixed.** Machines break down. If you happen to be around when this happens, don't just walk away and hope the next person will deal with it. A classic example of this is when the paper jams in a copier. Even if you didn't break it, take care of it.

Quibbling about blame and responsibility is always counterproductive and totally unprofessional.

- **If you don't know how to use it properly, learn.** Misuse of equipment is more than just a time-waster. It can also damage sensitive machinery. Pride is a silly – and often costly – thing to worry about in an office setting. Before you push that button or turn that dial, make sure you know exactly what you're doing – or ask for help.

- **When you're finished with it, make sure it's ready for the next person to use.** If you were making special copies on longer paper, or reducing the size of images, reset the copier when you are finished. Don't change computer programming or automatic dial numbers on the fax machine or phones without permission.

Stop and think the next time you use a piece of office equipment. Remember, it's not your possession to use as you wish. Exercising these four office courtesies can go a long way toward making your work environment pleasant and productive – and scoring points with your co-workers.

(7)

Don't be stupid about e-mails

Keep in mind, e-mails aren't private and they never disappear. Computer professionals can retrieve e-mails long after they've been deleted. If they appear on a company computer, they "belong" to the company. People can check them out at any time. Tell your friends to send jokes, chain letters, graphics, electronic greeting cards, etc., to your home computer.

E-mail guidelines to keep you from getting burned:

- **Know how to use your equipment and mail software** so you don't hit "reply" when you wanted to "forward."

- **Watch your words!** You may think that what you say is easy to understand, but sometimes words can be misconstrued. Be concise and to the point. This will eliminate the need for costly long-distance phone calls to follow up on e-mails that need further clarification.

- **Don't send negative comments, but delivering bad news is sometimes OK.** If you use antagonistic words or critical comments (known as "flames" in cyberspeak), it can hurt people and cause awkward situations.

E-mail is not the place to make negative comments. However, it can be a good way to avoid face-to-face encounters when bad news must be delivered. Typically, bad news is shared with more accuracy through an e-mail vs. an in-person encounter because no "sugarcoating" of the news is done – it's just the facts. Sometimes, however, delivering bad news in person is better. It shows that the messenger cares about the recipient's feelings.

- **Remember, few people like "spam."** When sending unsolicited e-mails, make sure that there is value to the recipient. If you don't, the person may very well consider it "spam," and delete it unread. Whenever possible, get the recipient's permission, or at least make sure that the person knows the e-mail is coming. Never try to make an unsolicited marketing e-mail look like official business – the strategy will backfire.

- **Nothing is private.** Even when a message is deleted, many software programs and on-line services can access messages on the hard drive. Before you click on "send," consider what may happen if the message is read by someone else – like the boss. The general rule of thumb is do not send personal or confidential e-mails at work (think twice about doing so even at home). Better safe than sorry. You certainly wouldn't want a client's secrets revealed or your off-color joke read by the wrong person.

- **Keep attachments to a minimum.** The larger the attached document, the longer it takes to download and the more memory space it fills on a recipient's computer. Some e-mail attachments may not be necessary. Consider faxing lengthy documents instead of using e-mail. Or, if time is not really an issue, use regular mail services, UPS or Federal Express.

- **CC or not to CC?** Just like a regular memo, you may want to send copies of your e-mail to others in the office or other clients. The same guidelines apply about flames and spams.

- **Never assume anything.** While you may be an Internet pro, and familiar with the lingo and emoticons like the popular smiley face :-) , don't assume the recipient is.

- **Think twice before hitting "reply to all."** When you are one of multiple e-mail recipients, consider who really needs to hear your response. It probably isn't necessary to hit the "reply to all" button. Most often, the original author of the e-mail is the only person to whom you need reply.

- **If your message doesn't need a response, let the recipient know.** This can save time – theirs and yours – and stop the cycle from continuing on in perpetuity. Say something like "No reply necessary" at the end of your message or even in the subject line.

- **Be careful about using e-mails to say only "Thank you" or "OK."** We said this before, but remember, it's OK to send some thank-you messages via e-mail – especially if that's how you normally correspond with the person. But, please say more than a word or two. One-word e-mail replies are no better than spam. Remember that, even in this digital age, nothing replaces an in-person thank-you message or handwritten note.

Some additional quick tips:

✓Use correct terms from start to finish.

✓ Don't be overly familiar, some may find it offensive.

✓ Always check before you click.

✓ Make sure that your tone is appropriate for the situation.

Managers should never use e-mails to lay off or fire people, and employees should never use e-mails to quit or resign. Hiding behind a monitor in these situations shows a lack of professionalism and common courtesy.

Above all, be careful about what you send. E-mails can spread like wildfire and end up in the wrong hands. Before hitting the send button, stop and think, "How would I feel if this e-mail ended up on the front page of *The Wall Street Journal?*" Or, even worse, "In my boss's in-box?"

CLM Flash: According to a survey by Microsoft Network, reported by BBC News, there are shocking lapses in e-mail etiquette for the under-25 crowd. The top four irritants reported were: lack of a formal greeting or sign-off, spelling mistakes, "overfamiliarity" and grammatical errors.

Grow Up!

(1)

Don't make me wait!

Being on time is a sign of respect. When you keep people waiting, it's irritating and makes others feel that you think you're more important. In our humble opinions, being late is one of the worst CLMs a person can make.

If tardiness is your rule rather than the exception, it's time to pay close attention to your clocks and watch. Time counts:

- when you are expected at work.

- when you are meeting someone.

- when you have to attend a meeting.

- when you have deadlines for assignments or projects.

Although some corporate cultures have time problems, it doesn't mean you should fall prey to them. Being consistently on time may just set you apart and give you an edge when it comes to special opportunities where reliability is critical.

Also, never assume that if you work for or with someone who isn't punctual that it is acceptable behavior. Clients and/or senior management certainly won't feel this way. When you ask for a certain amount of someone's time – for a meeting, advice or whatever – don't try to steal more than you requested.

You must take 100% responsibility for being on time. If there is a chance that traffic may be heavy on your commute to work, then get up earlier. If you're not sure where a meeting is being held, get clear directions and check them out well before you have to arrive.

Don't allow yourself to make excuses and you will save those you work with a great deal of aggravation. Be memorable because of your courteous, timely behavior. People are watching.

(2)

No more "all-nighters"

Have you ever found yourself saying, "I work better under pressure?" Is one of your favorite mottos, "Don't do today what you can put off till tomorrow?" If you answered yes to either of these, then chances are you suffer from being a procrastinator.

Occasionally in life you can do things at the last minute and manage by the seat of your pants. It really isn't the best way to approach a project, however, and often sends a message to others that you don't manage your time well.

Waiting until the last minute can also set you up for huge aggravation and potential failure. Consider this: You have been asked to complete a monthly report of your accomplishments vs. objectives. It is due Friday by noon because your manager has a meeting with the VP later in the afternoon to review the status of her department. You have waited until Friday morning to pull it together. Just as you start to collect the data, you get a call that you are needed immediately at a meeting to address a serious customer problem that just surfaced.

What are the chances that you will pull this one off? Even if you do, the quality of your report is likely to suffer, not to mention the terrible case of indigestion you are starting to develop. You may also find yourself so distracted by your dilemma that your ability to contribute at the client meeting is compromised. All in all, things don't look good for you.

Warning signs that you may be getting caught in the procrastination trap:

- **Overextending:** You take on multiple projects, then freeze when you realize it's more than you can handle. If this is the case, learn to be realistic about how much time things take. Occasionally, you might have to say "No" or at least delegate.

- **Fear:** When we are afraid, we can become paralyzed. The way to handle this is to acknowledge the fear and get started on the task at hand. Keep in mind that 90% of what you worry about never happens anyway. The 10% that does occur is rarely as bad as we thought it would be.

- **Liking the rush:** Some people thrive on crisis. Instead of creating that adrenalin rush at work, consider taking up some thrill-seeking sport or activity outside of the office.

- **Inability to delegate:** It's nice to think we can do it all, but the reality is that something always suffers – the quality of the work, your stress level or other factors. Learn to break projects into pieces and give away what you can.

- **Overwhelmed by the task:** It's best to approach every project as though you are eating an elephant – one small piece at a time. It makes the project much less daunting!

CLM Flash: "You cannot escape the responsibility of tomorrow by evading it today." – Abraham Lincoln

(3)

Have you cleaned your bedroom (uh, work space) yet?!

Your work space, like your clothing and grooming, says a lot about you as a professional. Therefore, it should be tidy and organized. If you can't locate an important file or information within minutes, rethink your organizational style.

When you're away – out sick or on vacation – other employees may need to access your office to find information. Don't leave your colleagues wondering if they should have had their shots before entering!

We're not suggesting that you have to be obsessive-compulsive, just reasonably together. How much is too much? Stacks of paper on the floor, no desk space showing, might be problems. It's a particular issue if your space is in the public view, or if others have to find information in your area. Managers may be concerned that assignments are going into a black hole.

Spend a day setting up files and systems that are easy to use – then use them!

Whether it's justifiable or not, your intellect and ability may be judged by the level of chaos or order that surrounds you at work.

Some level of organization will give you and your colleagues a sense of comfort and control.

(4)

Not everything is urgent

"There is no point doing well, that which you should not be doing at all."
– Thomas K. Connellan

Most people start to recognize early in their careers that not all things are equally important. However, recognizing this and doing something about it are two different matters.

Here are five questions to ask yourself when establishing priorities:

- What are your key objectives for the month, the week, the day?

- Which activities support your goals and which do not?

- Do you prioritize your "to do" list by completing important items first?

- Are you realistic about your ability to complete a task in a specific time period?

- Do other activities have a way of creeping in on your day? How relevant are these things to your objectives?

The night before or first thing each morning, stop and consider what is most important for you to accomplish on a specific day. Create a **prioritized** "to do" list. Commit yourself to completing those tasks first before other demands of the day creep in. This will give you focus. Also, don't be afraid to say, "No, I can't" or "Not today, but maybe tomorrow." Agree to do something if your manager has requested it and it is relevant to your position and objectives.

People who master the art of prioritization not only tend to accomplish more, especially of things that matter most; they also increase their odds of living a balanced life.

(5)

Life in the fast lane

If you drive to work rather than walk or take public transportation, pay attention to how you drive.

Do this not only for general courtesy and safety, but also because colleagues might see you. There's a good chance you may actually be driving the same route as many co-workers and could be in front of or behind them. Remember, the person who you believe is causing you grief may be a co-worker or customer. Don't be tempted to show your dissatisfaction with a rude gesture or by blowing your horn.

One of our clients shared a memorable, embarrassing moment with us. She was running late for an appointment with a new customer. Parking in the city of Boston where she worked was a nightmare. Her adrenalin was pumping as she jockeyed for a coveted spot, cutting off another contender in the process. The victim of her actions honked his horn. She responded with a rude gesture. You can imagine her horror when five minutes later she realized that the person she raised her middle finger to was the new customer she was meeting! We don't have to tell you that no business deal was made that day.

Help! Was That a Career Limiting Move?

Road rage is definitely a career limiting move! So what are the guidelines?

- Go the speed limit.
- Don't cut others off.
- Pay attention to stop signs, school zones and red lights.
- Avoid putting on makeup or doing other distracting things while driving (eating, shaving, etc.).
- Use a cell phone only when necessary, and use a hands-free device and/or when stopped.
- Don't turn your radio or CD player volume up so high that your windows vibrate and the cars next to you can make out the song's lyrics.
- Don't lose your cool over a parking space. There will always be another, and if it's further away, consider it an opportunity for a little more exercise. Never park in a space reserved for physically disabled drivers unless you have the required license plate or permit. Use only one parking space, even if you have a new car.

The way you maintain your car counts, too. You never know when you may be giving someone a ride and the appearance of your car (inside and out), just like your work space, says a lot about you. So…

- Keep it clean. Wash or have it washed regularly.
- Fix any fender benders.
- Keep the inside neat. Don't have dirt or litter anywhere.

(6)

Make it before you spend it

Early on in a career, being financially responsible is more personal than corporate. It's important to learn to manage your money wisely and demonstrate to others that you don't spend more than you make.

Money management may be tricky at times, and spending it is often tempting. Credit cards give us the ability to have and buy more than we should. Don't fall into the trap.

Discipline is key. Establish a budget that includes savings. If your company offers 401K participation or a savings plan, have the maximum deduction taken from your pay. If you don't have it, you won't spend it. The earlier you start saving, the better. You will form good habits and create long-term wealth and security.

If you are given a company expense account, treat it as though it was your own money. Keep good records and spend the money with a "return on investment" (ROI) approach.

Poor spending habits reflect directly on a person's judgment and maturity. Sporting the newest designer labels, driving flashy cars or socializing like a "high roller" can be seductive. The stress and worry created by spending beyond your means, however, will eventually show.

Nothing makes a person look better than the sense of calm and confidence that shows when everything, including your wallet, is truly "under control."

(7)

Sweat the small stuff

Have you ever heard the saying, "It's all in the details?" Yet often it's the details that get overlooked.

Details occur in everything we do – from the way we dress in the morning, proofread e-mail and other written documents, to how we manage time and return phone calls.

The individuals who take the time and make the effort to respect the seemingly "little things" in life set themselves apart.

When you earn the reputation as someone who pays attention to details, you also build …

- Trust – Others can count on you to be thorough and follow through on commitments in a timely and professional manner.
- Respect and appreciation – Individuals who take the time to remember little as well as big things show that they care about others. Customers and co-workers alike feel special and valued.

CLM Flash: "Little things don't mean a lot, they mean everything." – Unknown

(8)

Will they respect me in the morning?

Your behavior outside of traditional work hours and settings is as important as, if not more important than, what you do between 9 and 5 in your office.

There may be times when you will attend company-sponsored events (parties, picnics, conferences, etc.). You may also go out to lunch or dinner with colleagues and clients. These are opportunities for others to not only view your social graces, but your judgment as well.

Let's start with alcohol. To drink or not to drink, that is the question. In a word – *limit* your intake. Alcohol impairs judgment and can relax you too much. Our rule of thumb is have *one* drink if others are drinking and make sure it is accompanied by food. Depending on your physical size and tolerance level, you might be able to have two beers (in a Pilsner or comparable glass – please, no drinking directly from bottles) or two glasses of wine. However, it is much better to have one drink or a non-alcoholic beverage. Not only can it save you from potentially embarrassing yourself, but it also creates a better impression on the people around you. Don't feel as though you must drink alcohol. Soft drinks, water, iced tea, etc., are perfectly acceptable.

Grow Up!

Resist the temptation to model your behavior after the lowest common denominator, regardless of that individual's title. In other words, if a senior director starts to share off-color jokes or talks about people in the office or even clients in a demeaning or inappropriate way, don't follow suit! Keep your wits about you and your judgment. This is not the time or place to "let loose."

Never be lulled into believing that your words or actions at these events are "off the record." Invariably, someone will be watching *and* judging. Be disciplined and gracious and you can't go wrong. Save your wild and crazy side for college reunions or purely social gatherings of friends and family.

As we stated earlier, you *are* judged by the company you keep – so make sure that your spouse or friend who accompanies you understands these rules as well.

(9)

You want me to do *what*?!

Perhaps you have heard the old expression, "If you keep doing what you have been doing, you'll keep getting what you've been getting." At some point, you'll probably find yourself stuck or even obsolete.

That's why it is important to be open to new ideas. You don't need to embrace all new things instantly; that would be foolhardy. However, don't shut them out either. Innately, most people are resistant to change, but those who thrive on it tend to be able to do well in the current business climate.

Consider new opportunities and challenges in the context of your long-term goals. Don't be shortsighted. It has been said that successful people do those things that unsuccessful people are not willing to do.

Read, experiment, collect information and do analysis before making final decisions. New ideas, new directions, new options and experiences will continually be put in your path. Be ready and open to following them. Both the journey and the destination are likely to be far more rewarding.

(10)

I'd like to use a lifeline

A sign of strength is to admit your weakness. You don't have to know everything, but you do need to know where to get the necessary information or answers.

By asking others for help, you are really complimenting them – you are acknowledging their expertise. We don't mean you should continually bother people, or ask them repeatedly for some information. When you do ask, be polite, ask if the timing is good (or set up a better time), then take notes on what the person tells you. The notes keep you from repeatedly asking the same things and help ensure that you retain the information.

If people ask you something that you are unfamiliar with, don't lie. It's OK to say, "I don't know." Depending on the situation, you could say, "I don't know, however, I will find out and get back to you."

When in doubt, ask. If you don't, it could cost you a million dollars or something you can't put a dollar value on – your reputation!

(11)

Aw, you shouldn't have!

Giving gifts is often appropriate in a business setting, but it is very important to know when and how to give.

Here are some gifting guidelines.

- **When you are invited to someone's house for dinner:** A hostess (host) gift is appropriate. Good gift examples are: a plant, flowers sent in advance, wine (to be served at another time), an attractive calendar, a picture frame and scented soaps.

- **When you are invited to a colleague's wedding:** If you attend, a gift is required. If you don't attend, sending a gift is your choice – although always nice. The amount you spend on the gift depends on your pocketbook and your relationship to the person. Buy gifts from the registry, if appropriate.

- **When people at work give office parties to celebrate birthdays, showers, retirement, etc.** You shouldn't feel compelled to give a gift and it shouldn't be required. If you are a friend of the person, contribute to the group gift or say you want to give your own. If you really don't know or don't like the person, don't attend the party. If you do, give a congratulations card.

- **Holidays are a time for co-worker/boss gift giving.** If there are a lot of people, a "Pollyanna" or grab bag can keep down the cost of gifts and prevent feelings from being hurt. If you are special friends with someone, exchange gifts with this person after office hours. If your manager gives you a gift, it isn't necessary to reciprocate. You do need to write a thank-you note, however. If you do choose to give your manager a gift, you shouldn't spend the same amount, since he/she makes more money than you. There are lots of inexpensive but thoughtful gifts that people can give, including homemade foods, plants, candles, etc. Stay away from items that have religious connotations, unless you are sure that person practices the religion and wouldn't be offended by such gifts.

- **Holidays also are a time to give gifts to clients and vendors.** Always make sure you know what their company policy is, so you don't put them in a compromising or embarrassing situation. Once again, if you are the recipient of a gift from one of your vendors or clients, write a thank-you note. Business gifts always have to be in good taste – nothing too expensive or too personal.

(12)

Work hard/play hard

In today's 24/7 fast-paced work environment, it is hard to keep balance in your life. Granted, there are times when work will take precedence and other times when your personal life will, but overall, keeping balance is not only beneficial, it is smart. Here's how to keep the balance.

- **Set your limits and learn to say "No."** Your company will still be in business and you won't burn out.

- **Manage the expectations of your employer** by being clear on how your performance is measured and what your job priorities are.

- **Set time aside** to be with your family and friends, exercise, eat properly, sleep six to eight hours a night, and take a vacation or time off.

- **Do periodic sanity checks.** When was the last time you read a book or article that wasn't related to your job? Do you look forward to weekends as a time to be with family and friends or as extra hours without meetings to catch up on work-related projects?

Take time to enjoy activities and people who are completely independent of your job. You'll find the change of pace refreshing, and you are likely to become a more interesting person in the process.

You may be surprised to find that the art of balancing both work and play creates not only a happier you, but a more successful you as well. There is rarely an old person who, when reflecting on his or her life, says, "I wish I had spent more time working."

(13)

Whassup, Dawg?

Bad speech habits can be career killers. Whether you are fresh out of college with an "awesome" set of expressions or have acquired an abrasive accent or speech pattern -- like it or not, you probably will be judged accordingly.

Too often we see intellectually strong and capable people get labeled as less than they are because of how they speak. Here are some things to be mindful of.

Make sure that your language isn't peppered with "college speak." Being "dissed" by a co-worker or declaring that new assignment "way cool" sounds young and can interfere with your ability to gain respect.

Sloppy speech that leaves out details such as describing a meeting with "me and so-and-so," or giving an update on a project and finishing off with "blah, blah, blah," makes you look lazy and disinterested.

And of course as we've stated before, foul language is unacceptable in most work environments. Beyond offending some people's value system, cursing can lead the listener to believe 1) you have little or no respect for them and/or 2) you have such a limited vocabulary (i.e. little intelligence) that you're left with only words of the four-letter variety.

Make a commitment to clean up your speech before someone discounts you or your worth.

(14)

My bad!

Making, owning up to and learning from one's mistakes are an essential part of personal growth and success in the business world.

One of our favorite interview questions is this: "Tell us about a mistake you have made in your business life." Once the candidate has answered, we ask, "Was this the biggest mistake you have ever made?" We also ask what the candidate did about the mistake, the consequences and eventually, any lessons learned.

The answers to these questions are very revealing.

There was the candidate who couldn't give us an answer, even when gently prompted to take his time and come up with one. Warning! *No one* is perfect. No one is likely to have gone through life without making at least one business blunder.

The fact that this person couldn't come up with an answer revealed several possibilities, all not good: He was unable to acknowledge his own errors, which meant that he did not take responsibility for his mistakes and may have been likely to blame others; or the candidate had made mistakes, but chose not to be forthright in sharing any of them with us ... certainly not the foundation of an honest relationship; or he was unable to recognize, let alone acknowledge, his errors.

Needless to say, he didn't get the job.

What are HR directors and others who make hiring decisions seeking in a candidate? More than likely, the same thing most companies already expect of their employees – an honest acknowledgement of where they've gone wrong, where their responsibilities lay and how they will prevent the same mistake from being made in the future.

Most organizations are looking for individuals who are willing to take calculated risks, but who do so with accountability for their actions. So the next time you make a mistake (and you will), in addition to owning up to it by saying, "My bad," make sure you have the determination to pick yourself up and come away wiser ... and better prepared not to trip over the same thing in the future.

(15)

The dreaded pink slip

"You're fired!" It's an expression some have come to know through the TV show "The Apprentice," and one many have also experienced first hand. Typically the words come more like, "I'm sorry to tell you this, we need to make some cutbacks and ... ." Or, "We realize that this isn't working for you, and it isn't working for us either." Or perhaps, "You violated company policy, and we have no choice but to terminate your employment."

Choice of words aside, the ultimate message is still the same -- you no longer have a job at our company. Emotions ranging from devastated to discouraged may follow. The goal is to chart a new course for employment, one that not only brings a paycheck, but also offers professional satisfaction and success. The question is how?

First, take some time to reflect on what has happened. Is your termination a blessing in disguise? If so, why? What about your job and the company you worked for did you like and what didn't you like? What got you out of bed each morning, beyond the need to make money? Were there more positives than negatives, or was it vice versa? How did you feel about your manager?

Grow Up!

Taking the time to honestly answer these questions can help you learn more about yourself and identify what you care about in a work environment. The trick is to answer honestly without looking for excuses and ways to blame others. There is a difference between rationalizing away your own shortcomings or mistakes and understanding what you aren't good at or motivated by. The expression, "People do best what they love doing most" is true and powerful. Get clear on what this means for you.

Consider the contents of this book. How is your professional presence, your ability to communicate clearly and respectfully with others, your character and your knowledge of the industry in which you hope to work? What have you learned from the mistakes you made in the past? What are you going to do to increase your knowledge, skills or expertise in the areas you hope to work?

Don't bury your head in the sand just because you were let go, either in terms of self-awareness or in getting out and connecting with others. Networking can be one of the most powerful paths to finding your next opportunity. Along the way, strive to help others as well. Not only is it the right thing to do, it will establish you as someone who isn't just in it for selfish reasons alone.

Leave your past employer with dignity. By respecting the situation and position of those who had to make the difficult decision of letting you go, you may create important support and references down the road. No matter how hurt or angry you may be, channeling your energies in a way that displays empathy for all concerned, a desire to move forward in the right away and a dedication to contribute meaningfully to another organization will in time overshadow that dreaded pink slip.

(16)

It is what it is

"The world is not your mother."   -- Ghandi

Are there days when you wonder, "What were they thinking?!" as a directive comes down from above with a new company initiative, set of procedures or reports to be completed? Maybe it's an irritating co-worker who you feel isn't pulling his or her weight, but who seems to get recognized and rewarded all the time that makes you want to scream. Perhaps it's something more personal; you are working as hard as you can and it still doesn't seem like enough to your boss. Do you sometimes worry that your manager isn't as awe-inspiring as you'd always imagined or that you're being left alone to find your way and make mistakes?

The list of frustrations, inconsistencies and injustices that may occur in your work environment are endless. Too often, people use this as an excuse for their own failures or disengagement. The reality is that no environment (just like the people who work in them) is perfect. The other truth is that work is not there to serve you, but rather you are there to serve work.

Help! Was That a Career Limiting Move?

How can you make sure that you are a contributor and not a griper? Start by looking at your company, manager and work group in a constructive rather than critical way. Instead of complaining when you get home, give credit where credit is due, to people who have paid their dues, bring a unique talent or perspective to tasks at hand or who have wisdom and experience that perhaps you have yet to fully understand. Seek out individuals who you respect. Ask them to help give you the insight that you may not find on your own.

Look for ways that your intelligence, skills and insight can make something stronger. Find a way to create a presence that adds to your efforts and talent rather than subtracts from it. Don't let your own personal agenda, bias or need for attention be what drives you. You have been hired to help an organization be a competitive success, not to have your ego stroked or your purpose in life fulfilled.

Those who can go to work most days with happiness, passion and conviction are lucky. Those who do it with a balance of purpose and perspective on where they truly fit into the big picture of their organization are the most successful of all.

CLM Flash: Bill Gates gave a speech at Mt. Whitney High School in Visalia, CA. In it, he quoted author Charles Sykes by saying, "Life is not divided into semesters. You don't get summers off, and very few employers are interested in helping you find yourself. Do that on your own time."

It's All About Character

(1)

100% responsibility

Imagine what the world would be like if there was no blaming, no excuses, and everyone took 100% responsibility for their actions?

When we say 100% responsibility, we mean that each of us needs to accept total accountability – not just a part of it – for all commitments, relationships and actions.

If you are running late for work and someone in front of you is driving too slowly, don't blame this person for your tardiness. Take 100% responsibility to ensure that you don't oversleep or cut it so close that someone driving cautiously will make you late.

If you are asked to work on a team project and one of the members doesn't contribute on time, don't sit back and place blame. Take 100% responsibility to complete the task with or without the difficult teammate. Do what it takes to get the job done. You can assertively and helpfully confront the non-contributor. If that fails, work with the remaining team members to pick up the slack, finish the project and then address the issue with appropriate management.

Help! Was That a Career Limiting Move?

People who take 100% responsibility for their assignments and behavior spend time exploring options and opportunities, and are seen as more accomplished and trustworthy. The respect you will earn from others, plus the strength you will feel in controlling your own destiny, should more than make up for the extra effort, patience and diligence that 100% responsibility requires.

(2)

Honor thy commitments

In other words, do what you say you will. Think of people you know who keep their commitments, the ones who say they will help you, and do; the ones who say they will pick you up at 8 a.m. and arrive on time. Chances are that these are the same people you are most likely to count on and trust.

Dependable, trustworthy people are valued every bit as much in the work world as they are in our personal lives.

This doesn't mean saying "Yes" to everyone and everything. You must make commitments wisely and set priorities – but once you've made them, keep them.

What is your reliability quotient (RQ)? It may be more instrumental to your professional success than the other "quotient" you frequently hear about, your IQ.

(3)

It's not always about what you get

"Not thee who has much is rich, but thee who gives much." – Eric Frohm

Giving to charities is a great way to help others. Even though you might not be making a lot of money early on in your career, it is good to get in the habit of sharing your wealth. Many companies sponsor fund-raising efforts (walks/runs for AIDS or breast cancer research) or charitable organizations like the United Way or Red Cross. Donating money to charity is a good way for you to get company recognition and help those in need.

Of course, giving money is just one way to be charitable. How about donating your time by volunteering for good causes? Many companies encourage employees to get involved with local schools or activities like Big Brothers/Big Sisters of America or comparable organizations.

You can also put your athletic talents and experience to good use by organizing and participating in walks or runs for diabetes, breast cancer awareness and other important causes.

Being altruistic has lots of benefits. It puts you in the company of others who believe in the same causes that you do, which is helpful for mentoring and improving your social life. It also can build your sense of community and keep you grounded in some of the more important life lessons that can otherwise slip by. Finally, it can give you a sense of purpose and expand your skills and knowledge beyond the walls of your work environment.

CLM Flash: Let's build your word power. **Altruism** is the concern for the welfare of others. Challenge yourself to commit to at least one major cause (beyond your bank account or rising career), and make it a priority for your time, creativity and discretionary income.

(4)

You gotta deal with it

There are three things in life that are inevitable: death, taxes and change.

The way you do your job today will likely change, maybe next year, maybe next month, maybe tomorrow. The people you report to are also likely to change. The clients you have and the processes you use won't stay the same either. If you expect things to be the same, or to go as planned, you will inevitably be disappointed.

The key to survival is flexibility. Be able to go with the flow. The best ways to do that are:

- Manage your own expectations.

- Have a sense of humor.

- Expect the unexpected.

- Let go of perfectionist tendencies.

- Be open-minded in your opinions and willing to listen to differing views.

Here's an example of how a corporation effectively handled a major change: Leaders of a large pharmaceutical company recognized that changes in systems, management and corporate culture would result from an upcoming merger. They worked with their employees to teach them how **not** to be "victims" of change, but rather "navigators" through change.

Even if you are not as fortunate to work for a company with leaders who help empower you through change, take control yourself and find your own ways to grow and learn. Don't sit back and act powerless. This is an important lesson for us all in work and in life. View change as an opportunity and then seize it.

Above all else, remember that the one and only thing you can control about change is your attitude.

CLM Flash: "Change is certain, unless you are standing in front of a vending machine." – S. Holland

(5)

Diversity is not a spectator sport

Like it or not, we live in a world filled with different types of people. Your business environment most likely reflects this diversity. These differences add so much to the fabric of the organization, yet sometimes it may be difficult to appreciate them. This difficulty can be due to old stereotypes, lack of exposure to a variety of people and confusion as to how people think and act.

Diversity covers a variety of areas: age, race, religion, gender, national origin, socioeconomic background and education. People don't always see things the same way, or even have the same values, which can be confusing and frustrating. On the flip side, it can also be enlightening and very rewarding.

Our advice is to get to know people who are different from you. Be interested in what they value and the experiences that have shaped their perspectives and beliefs. Keep your mind open to the possibility that the way you see the world is not the only way to see it. Embrace the differences and work together with others who challenge you to look at situations in a way that you wouldn't have without them.

As you discover the benefits of appreciating diversity within your own organization, you will find that the lessons you learn may also have great value for situations you encounter with customers and others outside of your company.

Guaranteed, you will be a more enlightened and interesting person as a result.

(6)

"Optimism is a force multiplier." – Colin Powell

Given the choice, who would you rather be around – someone who is enthusiastic and has a positive outlook on the world or an individual who is apathetic at best and breathes doom and gloom at worst? Unless you are predisposed to masochistic tendencies, chances are you chose the former over the latter. You are not alone.

Not only are optimists more enjoyable to be around, their enthusiasm and positive outlook on life are more likely to generate successful outcomes in the working world.

We are not discounting the value of and need for rigorous thinking and healthy doses of realism. However, we have repeatedly seen that when individuals use their energy for solving problems vs. finding them, and are enthusiastic about doing so, their chances for success (not to mention happiness) are significantly greater.

How do you demonstrate enthusiasm? There are four ways.

- **Language:** The words you use should be positive and encouraging.

- **Body language:** Smile, gesture, have good eye contact.

- **Voice:** Have proper inflection and "punch."

- **Positive approach:** Direct your energy toward finding solutions and generating ideas and be prepared to focus on opportunities, rather than obstacles.

Enthusiasm is contagious and can fuel change, innovation and improvement in any organization. Optimism and enthusiasm sell. They sell our ideas and can sell us as individuals. Make sure your glass is half-full, rather than half-empty.

(7)

Integrity means doing the right thing
even when no one is looking

Have you ever been at the beach and picked up a handful of sand? Have you ever noticed that it's pretty easy to hold onto the sand until you let one grain slip out? All of a sudden, the remaining sand comes rushing out, no matter how hard you try to keep back the flow.

Some might say that this is a metaphor for holding onto integrity. Once you let some slip, it's more difficult to hold onto the rest.

Integrity can be your most valuable asset. Respect it, value it, honor it – by doing the right thing even when no one is looking.

(8)

It's nice to be important, but it's more important to be nice

"During my second month of nursing school, our professor gave us a pop quiz. I was a conscientious student and had breezed through the questions, until I read the last one: 'What is the first name of the woman who cleans the school?' I thought surely this was some kind of joke. I had seen the cleaning woman several times. She was tall, dark-haired and in her 50s, but how would I know her name? I handed in my paper, leaving the last question blank. Just before class ended, one student asked if the last question would count toward our quiz grade. 'Absolutely,' said the professor. 'In your careers, you will meet many people. All are significant. They deserve your attention and care, even if all you do is smile and say hello.' I've never forgotten that lesson. I've also never forgotten her name was Dorothy."

– A story told to us that we've never forgotten.

There's an old cliché that is as true today as it was 100 years ago: "Be nice to the people you meet on the way up, because you may meet them on the way back down."

Help! Was That a Career Limiting Move?

It's easy when you start working to want to please your manager or impress higher-ups in your company. This isn't a bad idea, if you are impressing others by doing your job, being pleasant, contributing to the bottom line and networking within the organization. It *is* a bad idea if you are doing it at the expense of others. You know what we mean – "sucking up" to more prominent individuals, but ignoring people you don't think will benefit you.

The magazine tycoon Malcolm Forbes once said there are no unimportant people. He respected the value and contributions of each individual within the organization.

Be interested in others. It's amazing how much you can learn and how you can make others feel important when you show an interest in them. Ask questions that evoke conversation, open-ended questions like, "How was your commute this morning?" If you know that the person has a child who plays soccer, inquire about the game. If someone has an ill parent, show concern. Take time to get to know people beyond what they do at work.

We all know the golden rule, "Do unto others … ." Therefore, if there is something you can do to help a colleague, do it. This doesn't mean you need to actually do his or her work, nor does it mean that you should be taken advantage of, but occasionally it is nice to use your spare time or talents to make life a bit easier for someone else. This fosters a team atmosphere among co-workers. It only takes one person to model these behaviors. It feels good to help others and chances are it will be contagious!

(9)

Make excellence a personal core value

Few would argue that there is any better example of a commitment to excellence than Tiger Woods, who made history when he won four consecutive majors. His example can help us more clearly define the concept of excellence that is so frequently boasted and bantered about, but which is still illusive in many ways and places.

We can sit mesmerized by an Olympic event in which the difference between a gold medal winner and someone who doesn't even place may be a mere .001 seconds or points. We can look to those who have excelled in their fields and get additional perspective on the "going above and beyond" elements of excellence.

Do not treat lightly your role in achieving excellence. Opportunities will present themselves each day. Be dedicated and prepared to take advantage of each opportunity in a way that demonstrates your personal commitment to this value.

"To do the right thing, at the right time, in the right way; to do some things better than they were ever done before; to eliminate errors; to know both sides of the question; to be courteous; to be an example; to work for the love of work; to anticipate requirements; to develop resources; to recognize no impediments; to master circumstances; to act from reason rather than rule; to be satisfied with nothing short of perfection."

– Marshall Field & Company's business philosophy

It bears repeating. Make excellence a personal core value!

CLM Flash: "Lots of people are good at what they do – the greatest ones know they can always do better." – Unknown

(10)

"Do what is right, do the best you can and treat others as you would like to be treated." – Lou Holtz

Lou Holtz, legendary football coach for Notre Dame, is today head football coach at the University of South Carolina. He is also a motivational speaker and author, and has a successful company, Holtz Enterprises LLC.

Overall, his record was 100-30-2 in 11 seasons at Notre Dame. He has built a reputation as one of the great coaches and motivators of the game.

His philosophy and motto, "Do what is right, do the best you can and treat others as you would like to be treated" has tremendous merit for work and play.

The next time you are uncertain about how to handle a difficult situation or you are tempted to act in a way that you know deep down is probably wrong, review Lou's three rules. Use them as a checklist, a sanity check and when needed, as a moral compass. Odds are, you will be very glad that you did.

Learning the Hard Way

CLMs we've found in our travels

(1)

There are no unimportant people

Allison couldn't believe her good fortune! While at a woman's networking session, she found herself seated at the same table as Beth, the Director of Human Resources for their employer – a large aerospace company.

Allison had been with the firm for two years, joining it in a marketing communications position – but her degree was in human resources and she had been waiting for an opportunity in this department to become available. Allison felt this would be a place to put her degree and talents to better use.

During the dinner, she and Beth struck up a conversation and discovered that they had many things in common. They both were avid skiers and had been raised in the northwest, near Seattle. Allison also learned that a posting for a human resource manager was scheduled to go up that Friday. Allison left the dinner in high spirits and with an invitation to meet at Beth's office the following Tuesday to discuss the position and other career opportunities.

Allison and her roommate shared high fives when she returned to her apartment. Allison couldn't have planned for a better break – she felt comfortable, bordering on smug. She felt that she had her foot in the door and an edge over any possible competition.

Help! Was That a Career Limiting Move?

When Tuesday came, Allison arrived at Beth's office five minutes before her appointment. Beth's administrative assistant, Susan, looked frazzled. There had been some confusion with Beth's schedule and Susan was not prepared for Allison's visit.

Allison was indignant. Her tone with Susan reflected annoyance and impatience. "Beth is expecting me," Allison said, "she and I planned this meeting last week at dinner. We're personal friends, so please get this straightened out." When Susan apologetically asked if she could reschedule the appointment for the following week, Allison refused and insisted that she speak with Beth without delay.

Susan disappeared into Beth's office with a heavy sigh. Moments later, Beth appeared and graciously escorted Allison into her office. They were together a mere 15 minutes. Allison felt the tension, but rationalized that it was due to Beth's crazed schedule.

One week later, Beth called and informed Allison that she was not a final candidate for the open Human Resources Manager position. Beth explained that as an HR manager, Allison would need to make everyone feel equally respected and appreciated. Given the way Allison treated her administrative assistant, Beth felt Allison didn't have the maturity or character traits necessary to be a successful member of her team.

(2)

Be careful with bathroom banter

Michael was a newly hired sales rep at a pharmaceutical firm. His training and that of his fellow new reps consisted of three weeks of intensive study at the home office.

The training culminated in physician role-play situations where the new sales consultants were required to use appropriate promotional materials and "detail" the MDs on the benefits of their products. Because everyone was videotaped during these mock sales sessions, the tension was usually quite high.

On the day of this role play, Michael – and others in his class – decided to take a quick bathroom break 10 minutes before their taped exchange was to happen. While in the bathroom stall, he heard someone next to him who he believed was suffering from gastrointestinal distress.

Michael reached under the stall, patted the ankle of his bathroom neighbor, and reassuringly stated, "Hey buddy – don't get so uptight about this. It's just a role play. What are they going to do if we screw it up? It's not like they'll fire us or anything!"

Help! Was That a Career Limiting Move?

You can imagine Michael's horror when he stepped out to wash his hands and suddenly realized the person he'd comforted was not a fellow trainee, but rather the Vice President of Sales for the company!

(3)

Being inconsiderate ... guaranteed to blow your chances

A semiconductor company was in the process of hiring a senior level engineer. The interview process had resulted in the selection of a final candidate whose experience, degree and unique skill set appeared to be a solid match.

The final step of the process for anyone joining the company was for the person to go through psychometric testing. This was conducted by an independent organization who administered a number of instruments designed to assess whether there was a fit between the personal characteristics of a candidate and the company's culture and values.

The engineering candidate arrived at the testing center as planned – but with a terrible head cold. He asked for a box of tissues, which were promptly brought to him in the conference room, along with a cup of coffee he'd also requested.

When the testing center called the semiconductor company at the end of the day, the conversation went like this: "Steve, before we give you John's specific test results, you need to know that after John finished, and was gone, we discovered that he had left bunched up, dirty tissues along with his empty coffee cup and stirrer on our mahogany conference table."

Result – the findings of the psychometric testing were irrelevant. John did not have the basic social skills or consideration for others necessary to be offered the job.

(4)

Whether you have a dog or not …

Two individuals from a recruiting company – the president and an account manager – were dining out at an upscale restaurant with a prospective client, a decision maker from a large corporation.

When the meal was finished, the waiter asked all three if they wanted their leftovers wrapped. The president declined, as did the prospect.

The account manager, however, said, "I'll have mine wrapped up, and since he's (pointing to the prospect) not taking his, I'll take it." The waiter took both plates and returned with two carefully wrapped foil packages. The account manager took the packages and said to his two stunned dining companions, with a bit of a chuckle, "Waste not, want not."

The president was mortified, but couldn't say anything at the time for fear of embarrassing the account manager and further calling attention to an already uncomfortable situation.

In the weeks following this dinner, the results of the "doggy bag" incident were obvious – the recruiting firm did NOT get the business.

(5)

Remember your audience

Last year, we were in the middle of a recruitment and selection process for a new account manager at Brody Communications Ltd. Marjorie was part of the final interview process as we narrowed our selection down to three potential candidates. John successfully answered many of the questions being thrown at him. At one point, the conversation turned to the subject of his love of and interest in training.

When we asked, "Did you ever consider a career in education?," he glibly responded, "Oh no, I wasn't interested. You know the old saying, 'Those who can, do, and those who can't, teach.'"

John said this, completely overlooking the fact that Marjorie's first career was as a college professor and that the entire essence of our company is centered on the value of teaching.

Although he called back later that afternoon to apologize – when he'd realized what he said – the damage was already done. The issue was not Marjorie's ego in this case, but rather John's lapse of judgment and lack of appreciation for who we are and what we do. His comments revealed his true thoughts and opened our eyes to why he was certainly not a fit for our company.

(6)

Those who need it the most may recognize it the least

Linda, an account manager at Brody Communications Ltd., was thrilled to get a call from a large financial consulting firm that was interested in our services for business etiquette training. She was told that she would need to present our capabilities to four decision makers representing different departments within the company.

During the subsequent meeting, Linda distributed our materials and spoke about the hidden costs of unprofessional behavior. At points during her presentation, she found it difficult to concentrate because one gentleman in the group, Larry, clipped his fingernails the entire time. As appalling as it may sound, he even picked his nose twice!

At the end of her presentation, as three of the decision makers discussed how to move forward, the nail-clipping, nose-picking client blurted out, "There are better ways for me to spend my money. We don't need a course in manners."

Despite Larry's resistance, Brody Communications was hired to conduct an etiquette program. The following month, when we returned to conduct this first training session, he was no longer with the company.

(7)

Proper preparation shows you care

Bob was celebrating his 30th anniversary with a large pharmaceutical company. As was the firm's tradition, he was recognized during a celebration in one of its large conference rooms. In Bob's case, more than 60 people had gathered to pay tribute and eat cake.

His new supervisor, Tom, was responsible for delivering a toast and a brief review of Bob's key accomplishments and history with the firm. Everyone gathered knew how important Bob's career was to him. They also knew that he had just gone through a rather difficult and messy divorce.

As Tom raced into the room a little late, he began his toast to Bob with these words: "A good, long-term relationship with a company is like a good marriage. You're married, Bob, right?" and then proceeded to build his entire tribute around the relationship/marriage theme. Not only was everyone in the room embarrassed and uncomfortable for Bob, but the Vice President of Human Resources, turned to one of the other executives and said, "looks like Tom is going to need some significant coaching and feedback."

Bob was not the only victim of this CLM. The company probably lost a measure of respect and loyalty that day from everyone in the room. Why? Because the company allowed someone to be in a management role who obviously didn't take the time to know and appreciate the individual who was being honored.

That supervisor represented the company that day … and fell short of reflecting the kind of respect and understanding of what Bob meant to the business.

(8)

Nobody respects a cheat

Brett had worked as an account executive at an advertising agency for two years. One morning, he received a call from his boss asking how good his golf game was. Brett replied, "Not bad, and I love playing." "Terrific," said his supervisor, "the president needs someone within the company to complete his foursome for a charity golf tournament on Friday."

Brett was thrilled – a Friday of golf and a chance to have some personal attention from the company president! He polished his clubs, carefully chose his best golf attire for the day, and prepared himself for a winning afternoon. All was going well until the eighth hole, when Brett sliced the ball on a drive and it landed in the rough. Embarrassed by his sloppy swing, the fact that his game was not up to par, and that he felt he was already holding his foursome back, this most recent shot only made matters worse.

As they approached the fairway, Brett had a plan. He decided to discreetly move his ball out of the rough into a better position. So when no one was looking, he kicked it a couple of feet closer to the green. Certain that no one had seen what he did, Brett relaxed and continued playing golf, fairly well.

The players gathered for drinks after the game. The president took Brett aside, and said, "I saw you move the ball on the eighth hole. I'm disappointed in your actions. Remember this, Brett: 'A poor golfer is better than a dishonest employee.'"

We can be certain that any level of trust Brett had earned with the company was damaged that day.

(9)

Model the behaviors you want others to follow

A company had decided that one of its training priorities was to hold a time management course. After exploring alternatives to deliver this program, they carefully selected a local training firm whose array of offerings included this topic.

It was determined that this program would coincide with a regularly scheduled "lunch and learn session" and would last 45 minutes. Believe it or not, on the day of the session, the trainer actually arrived 15 minutes late for her time management course. Her excuse? Her watch had stopped.

Result? The training firm lost a client. The trainer lost her job.

(10)

People won't hear what you say if they're distracted by how you look

We walked into a client's office minutes after Janice, the manager of information technology services, had given a presentation to 50 of her fellow employees. Coincidentally, we had been invited there to discuss presentation skills training.

It was clear from the people we met that they were still abuzz about the morning's events. Everyone was talking about Janice's presentation.

Naturally, we were curious why. We asked a few of those in attendance what made her presentation so noteworthy. They explained that Janice had worn a beautiful, white summer suit. The only problem was that she was also wearing red, bikini underwear that could clearly be seen through the skirt. After sharing in their amusement/horror, we asked what her talk was about. After a few seconds of silence, and a nervous laugh or two, someone finally spoke up and said, "You know what, I don't remember."

Lesson here: A full body check in front of a mirror before leaving the house each day is essential to ensure a professional image.

(11)

Sending gifts … it really is the *thought* that counts

Jay was a fast-rising executive with a financial consulting firm. He was known throughout the organization as someone who was dedicated, bright and extremely well read.

It was not uncommon for Jay to give books as gifts to those who worked for and with him.

One January, we received a concerned call from the director of human resources at Jay's company. That year, Jay had, in his customary fashion, given out a book as a holiday gift to every staff member. A major section of this book, however, advocated Christianity.

Those on Jay's staff who were not of the Christian faith found the book disturbing. They questioned whether Jay was trying to promote his own faith, or if he had merely and carelessly given out a book that he had not found time to read. Neither answer was acceptable.

(12)

Habla "Oops?"

Carlos and Gina had just made their best sales call of the month. They had decided to visit a key customer together. Carlos discussed the cost effectiveness of using their product, and Gina reviewed the advantages of her company's technology.

The customer showed a great deal of interest, and asked that a specific proposal be sent to him by the end of the week. This was a major coup – if Carlos and Gina could gain this business, it would mean beating out the competition, who had a five-year foothold in the company.

As they stepped onto the elevator, it was very crowded. Anxious to continue strategizing about their proposal, Carlos and Gina decided to carry on their conversation in Spanish. They commented on how shocked their competition was going to be.

When they reached the lobby and stepped off the elevator, one gentleman called out to them, also in Spanish. "Don't be so certain of your victory just yet," he said.

Turns out he was the sales representative from the competing company! Guess who didn't get the business after all?

(13)

On top of spaghetti ...

Many times when we are called in to conduct an executive coaching engagement, it is to help an individual strengthen some element of communication, leadership and management skills, or overall professional presence. Typically, the person has made measurable contributions to the organization and is being groomed for a position of greater influence and authority.

Recently we were with a client who shared the story of a doomed executive, someone for whom coaching was no longer an option. Apparently, this guy had earned the unshakable reputation of being inconsiderate and unreliable.

At issue was his habitual tardiness, and personal excuses that not only didn't make up for being late, but also called into question his judgment and authority at home. Beyond that, he had created quite a stir by rolling up the leg of his pants in a meeting, exposing his hairy leg and asking for an impromptu diagnosis of a spot on his calf.

But the "pièce de résistance," the action that perhaps sealed his fate, was the elevator incident. This man carried a plate full of spaghetti back from the company cafeteria to his office. Along the way, he spilled a fair amount of it in the elevator as witnessed by several employees. To their shock, he kept going and never even attempted to clean up his mess -- a final punctuation mark to the lack of consideration and respect for others that had become his trademark.

CLMs of the rich and famous

Help! Was That a Career Limiting Move?

There are some who think that if they reach a high enough position or earn enough money, they can pass some magical threshold where immunity from career limiting moves is granted. It is a dangerous and false assumption to make. Let's take a look at a few who have made headlines recently as a reminder that even if you are rich and/or famous, the teachings of this book still apply.

On March 31, 2003, Peter Arnett was fired by NBC news. The reason -- Peter went on an Iraqi TV station and publicly demeaned the United States, saying in an interview that he felt that the U.S. military had failed during the early stages of the Iraqi war. Outrage from the American public came because Peter was seen as non-supportive of American troops by sharing his views on an enemy's propaganda show.

However, through the eyes of Peter's employer, NBC, the situation called for an additional perspective. Regardless of political or philosophical beliefs, NBC saw it this way: They had paid Mr. Arnett a salary and travel expenses to report accurately and objectively on the Iraqi war. He was paid by NBC to do a job, not promote his own personal agenda on company time on an opposing network -- end of discussion. Mr. Arnett was out of work.

What about Martha Stewart? Whether you believe she got a bad deal or that she got just what she deserved -- the lesson is still the same. If you get greedy or think that your title somehow puts you above the law, think again. You may reach a point where you sit at the head of the table in the boardroom, but the same principles of honesty and integrity apply to you. As a matter of fact, as someone in a leadership or high visibility role, it can be argued that your responsibility to exemplify those qualities becomes even greater.

Finally, let's look at the Enron senior executive team -- a study in both corruption and courage. While the consequences for the individuals involved are still unfolding, career lessons abound. Don't let the hierarchy of an organization replace your conscience. In other words, if you are in a position where you are clearly exposed to wrong doings, don't rationalize the unethical behavior away just to keep your job and salary. In the end, you will sacrifice a whole lot more.

About Brody Communications Ltd.

Brody Communications Ltd. works with employees at Fortune 500 companies and other organizations to sharpen their communication skills to boost performance.

For more than 20 years, Brody Communications has helped individuals and organizations reach new levels of professional success. Our firm can focus a training program or workshop to fit your particular audience and your specific situation.

Brody Communications Ltd. is certified as a Women's Business Enterprise.

Any Brody Communications account representative can send you program outlines, sample materials, or meet with your group about any Brody offering.

Call 800-726-7936 today to find out how Brody Communications Ltd. can create a difference for your bottom line!

Sharpening Communication Skills to Boost Performance™

Career Enhancing Books

I want to buy another *Help!* book for someone I know, $14.95 _____

Career MAGIC: A Woman's Guide to Reward & Recognition (hardcover), $24.95 ____

Speaking is an Audience-Centered Sport (3rd edition), $24.95 _____

*Professional Impressions ... Etiquette for Everyone, Every Day
(3rd edition), $19.95* _____

21st Century Pocket Guide to Proper Business Protocol, $19.95 _____

Market Your MAGIC: A Guide to Reward & Recognition, $14.95 _____

Life Without Limits: A Guidebook to Turning Your Dreams Into Reality, $19.95 ____

I live in PA, please charge me 6% tax, or 7% if I live in Philadelphia _____

TOTAL* _____

does NOT include shipping & handling charges, which will vary depending on weight and location shipped.

I want to pay with (circle one) Visa   MasterCard   American Express   Check   Money Order

Credit Card number _____ Expiration _____ CV2# _____

Name _____ Company _____

Address _____ City/State/Zip _____

Phone Number _____ Add me to your Ezine list _____